THE**REP**
Birmingham Repertory Theatre

Birmingham Repertory Theatre Company presents

Cling To Me Like Ivy

by Samantha Ellis

First performed at The Door, Birmingham Repertory Theatre
on 11 February 2010

The subsequent tour is supported by the
Sir Barry Jackson Trust

This play was developed with the support of the
European Association for Jewish Culture

Supported by
THE
SIR BARRY JACKSON
TRUST

European Association
for Jewish Culture

www.jewishcultureineurope.org

Cling To Me Like Ivy
by **Samantha Ellis**

PATRICK	Gethin Anthony
MALKA	Amanda Boxer
LEELA	Mona Goodwin
SHMULEY	Edward Halsted
DAVID	David Hartley
RIVKA	Emily Holt

Director	Sarah Esdaile
Designer	Ruari Murchison
Lighting Designer	Simon Bond
Composer	Simon Slater
Sound Designer	Clive Meldrum
Casting Director	Julia Horan
Assistant Director	Katie Henry
Choreographer	Nick Winston
Dramaturg	Caroline Jester

Stage Manager	Richard Watson
Deputy Stage Manager	Gabriel Bartlett

With special thanks to
Hannah Boyden
Ben Margolis
Rev Lionel Rosenfeld

Cast

Gethin Anthony (PATRICK)

Gethin graduated from LAMDA last summer, where he played Michael Digmore in the world premiere of Mark Ravenhill's *On the Boost*. Theatre credits include: *What Fatima Did* (Hampstead); *Fairytaleheart* (Old Red Lion); *The Death of Cool* (Tristan Bates); *Ready/24 Hour Plays* (Old Vic); *Cyrano de Bergerac, Europe, As You Like It, Three Sisters* (Oxford Playhouse/OUDS). Television credits include: *10 Days to War, Doctors, Pinochet's Progress, Holby City*. Radio credits include: *Legsy Gets a Break*. Film credits include: *Into the Storm, Farringdon Smith, Beyond the Rave*.

Amanda Boxer (MALKA)

Amanda was born in New York and trained at LAMDA. Theatre credits includes: *Many Roads to Paradise* (Jermyn Street); *Many Roads to Paradise, The Destiny Of Me* (Finborough); *The Last Days of Judas Iscariot* (Almeida); *The Pain and the Itch, The Strip* (Royal Court); *An Ideal Husband, The Rivals* (Theatr Clwyd); *Dis-Orientations* (Riverside Studios); *The Arab-Israeli Cookbook* (Gate/Tricycle); *Angel* (Shadow Factory); *A Small Family Business* (West Yorkshire Playhouse); *Macbeth* (Arcola); *The Graduate* (Gielgud); *The Yiddish Queen Lear* (Bridewell/Southwark Playhouse); *Iphigenia in Aulis* (Southwark Playhouse); *The Holocaust Trilogy* (New End); *A Touch of the Poet* (Young Vic/Comedy); *The House of Bernarda Alba* (Globe); *All My Sons, The Merchant of Venice, The Importance of Being Earnest* (Young Vic); *The Fall Guy, The Misanthrope, Absurd Person Singular, Present Laughter, Come Blow Your Horn* (Royal Exchange, Manchester); *Secret Rapture, Death and the Maiden* (Library Theatre, Manchester); *Lady Windermere's Fan* (Wolsey Ipswich). Amanda won Best Actress in the 1992 London Fringe Awards for Martha in *Strange Snow*. Television credits include: *Doctors, Bodies III, The Shell Seekers, Casualty, Tom Brown's School Days, Trial and Retribution III and VII, The Ruth Rendell Mysteries – Road Rage, Unnatural Pursuits, Inspector Alleyn Mysteries, Cider with Rosie, Goodbye My Love, In Suspicious Circumstances*. Film credits include: *Malice in Wonderland, Together, Chatroom, United 93, Les Poupes Russes, Sorted, Saving Private Ryan, Bad Behaviour, Nostradamus*.

Mona Goodwin (LEELA)

Mona graduated from Mountview Academy of Theatre Arts, Acting course. Since graduating, Mona has worked with Theatre503, filmed an episode of *Doctors* (BBC), worked on the film *Freefall* for Dominic Savage, and was in the highly successful *Spring Awakening* which transferred from the Lyric Hammersmith to the West End. She comes straight from playing Lakshmi in *The Jungle Book* (Castle Theatre, Wellingborough). Mona has just finished filming a remake of *Brighton Rock* for director Rowan Joffe, due for release late 2010.

Edward Halsted (SHMULEY)

Theatre credits include: *A Little Neck* (Hampton Court Palace); *Macbeth* (Big Stage Productions); *Aladdin* (Marlowe, Canterbury); title role in *Faust* (Punchdrunk/National Theatre); *Firebird Ball* (Punchdrunk); *Josephine* (Oldham Coliseum and tour); *Sisters and Others* (Scarlet Theatre); *Dreams of Anne Frank* (Polka); *Bartleby* (Red Shift Productions) for which he won the Best Actor Award at Edinburgh; *Single Spies* (National Theatre and West End); *Death of a Salesman* (Nottingham Playhouse); *Gloo Joo* (Hampstead/Criterion); *Shadowlands* (Carnival); *Sherlock's Last Case* (Salisbury Playhouse); *Macbeth*, *The Merchant of Venice* (St George's); *Outside Edge* (Plymouth Theatre Royal); *Dreyfus*, *The Tribades* (Hampstead); *Phantom of the Opera* (Actors' Company); *King Lear* (Cork Opera House); *Action Replay* (Orange Tree, Richmond); *James Joyce and the Israelites* (Lyric Hammersmith); *Someone Who'll Watch Over Me* (Dukes, Lancaster); *The Marriage of Mr Mississippi* (New End); *Little Eyolf* (Bird's Nest); *Beat the Air* (Finborough); *Next Time I'll Sing to You* (Millstream); *Julius Caesar* (Belgrade, Coventry); *Gaslight* (Channel); *Simon at Midnight* (Young Vic). Television credits include: *MI High, Not Going Out, The Bill, Jonathan Creek, Kavanagh QC, Brookside, The Nation's Health, Brothers and Sisters, The Bill, Boot Street Band, 99-1, Van Der Valk, A Very British Coup, The Vicar of Dibley, Picking Up the Pieces, Fish, The House of Eliott, Gloo Joo*. Film credits include: *Clive Hole, The Misanthrope, Leon the Pig Farmer, Dinner in Purgatory, Soho Sunset*. Radio credits include: *Whitechapel Dreams, Like They've Never Been Gone* (four series), *Church Ladies, Shadowlands*.

David Hartley (DAVID)

Theatre credits include: *The Tempest* (York Theatre Royal/Sprite Productions); *I Caught Crabs in Walberswick* (High Tide Festival); *Lovely and Misfit* (Trafalgar Studios); *If I Were You* (Stephen Joseph); *Holes* (Nuffield, Southampton); *Measure for Measure* (Globe/USA Tour); *Edward II* (Sheffield Crucible). Television credits include: *The Bill, Doctors, Talk to Me, Kingdom, The Amazing Mrs Pritchard*.

Emily Holt (RIVKA)

Cling To Me Like Ivy is Emily's theatrical debut after leaving LAMDA last summer. On graduating from LAMDA she was cast in *The Pillars of the Earth*, a new TV series adapted from Ken Follett's best selling novel (Tandem and Scott Free Productions). Theatre at LAMDA includes: *The Permanent Way, On the Boost* (premiere of a new Mark Ravenhill play), *Passport to Pimlico, New England*. Theatre prior to LAMDA includes: *Cabaret* (Lyric Hammersmith); *The Far Pavilions* (Shaftsbury); *Grease* (UK tour). Film includes: *The Boat That Rocked*.

Creative Team

Samantha Ellis (Writer)
Samantha Ellis's plays include *Patching Havoc* (Theatre503); *A Sudden Visitation of Calamity* (Menagerie at the Junction); *Startle Response* (Young Vic workshop); *Sugar and Snow* (Hampstead and BBC Radio 4); *Martin's Wedding* (with Blind Summit, at BAC); *Use Me As Your Cardigan* (Jackson's Lane), *Feel the Plastic* (Camden People's Theatre), and, for the Miniaturists, *Cat in a Sieve* (Southwark Playhouse), *Scattering* (Arcola) and *Unfinished* (Liverpool Everyman). She was a MacDowell Colony Fellow in 2008 and has worked as a journalist and editor for the *Guardian*, *Observer*, *TLS*, *Prospect*, *Jewish Quarterly* and the BBC. She wrote *Cling To Me Like Ivy* while on attachment at Birmingham Repertory Theatre. She is currently writing a play for LAMDA, and is on attachment at the Hampstead Theatre.

Sarah Esdaile (Director)
Sarah's directing credits include: co-directing Philip Pullman's *His Dark Materials* (Birmingham Repertory Theatre and on tour) with Rachel Kavanaugh; *Life X 3* (The Watermill); *The Horse Marines* (Drum, Plymouth); *Drowning on Dry Land* (Salisbury Playhouse); *Kafka's Dick* (Watford Palace); *The Grouch* (West Yorkshire Playhouse); *James and the Giant Peach* (Bolton Octagon), M.E.N Award, Best Family Show 2007; *Crocodile Seeking Refuge* (tour); *Lysistrata* (Arcola); *Pictures of Clay* (Royal Exchange, Manchester); Young people's *Taming of the Shrew* (RSC); *Compact Failure* (Clean Break, Arcola and tour); *Coyote on a Fence* (Royal Exchange, Manchester/Duchess, West End), M.E.N Award Best Fringe Production 2004; *The Maiden's Prayer* (Bush); *See How Beautiful I Am* (Bush/Pleasance, Edinburgh); *Bill and Esme* (Chelsea); *The Woolgatherer* (BAC); *The Boys Next Door* (Latchmere); *Downtown Paradise* (Finborough/Chapter Arts Centre, Cardiff); *Flip* (Hen and Chickens); *Resistance* (Old Red Lion); *Loot* (Thorndike, Leatherhead). As Assistant Director: *Troilus and Cressida*, *A Month in the Country* (RSC); *Henry V, The Merchant of Venice*, *A Chaste Maid in Cheapside* (Globe). Sarah was also an Associate Director at the RSC on Michael Boyd's Olivier-Award-winning productions of *Henry VI Part I, II* and *III*, and *Richard III*. Future work includes: *Death of a Salesman* (West Yorkshire Playhouse).

Ruari Murchison (Designer)
Ruari has designed productions in Helsinki (Finland); Washington DC; The Stratford Festival (Canada); Stuttgart (Germany); Luzern (Switzerland); Haarlem (Holland); Elsinore (Denmark) and many regional theatres in the United Kingdom. Theatre design credits include: *Mappa Mundi, Frozen, The Waiting Room, The Red Balloon* (National Theatre); *Titus Andronicus* (RSC); *Othello* (Trafalgar Studios); *The Solid Gold Cadillac* (Garrick); *A Busy Day* (Lyric, Shaftsbury Avenue); *Peggy Sue Got Married* (Shaftsbury); *The Snowman* (Peacock); *Toyer* (Arts); *3 Sisters on Hope Street, The Glass Room, Gone To LA* (Hampstead); *Henry IV, Part I* and *II* (Washington Shakespeare Company, USA); *West Side Story, The Sound of Music* (Stratford Festival, Canada); *Hamlet* (Elsinore, Denmark); *Macbeth, Electricity, Medea, The Lion, the Witch and the Wardrobe, Alice in Wonderland, Othello* (West Yorkshire Playhouse); *Mrs Warren's*

Profession, *The Threepenny Opera, An Enemy of the People* (Theatr Clwyd); *His Dark Materials, Uncle Vanya, The Life of Galileo, A Doll's House,* the David Hare Trilogy (*Racing Demon, Absence Of War, Murmuring Judges*), TMA Best Design Nomination 2003; *The Tempest, Macbeth, The Merchant of Venice, Hamlet, Frozen, Jumpers, Nativity, A Wedding Story, His Dark Materials* (Birmingham Repertory Theatre); *Intemperance, Tartuffe* (Everyman and Playhouse, Liverpool); *Copenhagen, Alfie* (Watford Palace); *Glamour* (Nottingham Playhouse); *Tartuffe* (Rose, Kingston); national tours of *His Dark Materials, Othello, Twelfth Night, Hamlet, The Merchant of Venice, Romeo and Juliet, A Wedding Story, A Doll's House, Dracula, Little Sweet Thing, The Snowman.*
Opera credits include: *Der Freischütz* (Finnish National Opera); *Peter Grimes, Così fan Tutte* (Luzerner Opera, Switzerland); *La Cenerentola, Il barbiere di Siviglia* (Garsington); *L'Italiana in Algeri* (Buxton); *Les Pelerins de la Mecque, Zaza* (Wexford). Ballet credits include: *Bruise Blood* (Shobana Jeyasingh Dance Company); *Landschaft und Erinnerung* (Stuttgart Ballet, Germany); *The Protecting Veil* (Birmingham Royal Ballet).

Simon Bond (Lighting Designer)
Simon is a Lighting Technician at Birmingham Repertory Theatre. Recent designs for The REP include: *The Writing on the Wall, What the Dickens, Long Lost, 8sixteen32, Looking for Yoghurt, Three Way, 2 Young 2 Luv, These Four Streets, Speckled Monster* (at Birmingham Thinktank), *Henry VI* and *The Mothership.*

Simon Slater (Composer)
Simon has composed original music for over 200 theatre, film, television and radio productions. Simon has just written the music for the highly successful *Two Men of Florence* by Richard N Goodwin (Huntington, Boston) directed by Ed Hall, and, in 2010, wrote original music for *Romeo and Juliet* (RSC) directed by Neil Bartlett, which had a packed-out tour of England and a season at Stratford. Other recent work includes: original music for *Kafka's Dick* (Watford Palace); *The Grouch* (West Yorkshire Playhouse); the award-winning *James and the Giant Peach* (Bolton Octagon); *Coyote on a Fence* (Royal Exchange, Manchester/Duchess, West End), all directed by Sarah Esdaile. Other recent projects include: *Beachy Head* for the award-winning Analogue Theatre Company; *Becoming Marilyn* (Edinburgh Festival 2009); *Mad Forest* (BAC); *Ones That Flutter* (Theatre503); *James and the Giant Peach* (Watermill, Newbury); and original songs for *The Wizard of Oz* (Winchester Theatre Royal). Simon has written the music for *Henry V, Julius Caesar* (RSC); *Macbeth* (Albery, West End); *For Services Rendered* (Watermill, Newbury). He was the musical supervisor on *Rose Rage* (Chicago Shakespeare Theatre and the Dukes Theatre, New York), all directed by Ed Hall. Other theatre music includes: *Honour* (Wyndham's, West End); the multi-award-winning *Mile End* for Analogue Theatre Company. Television credits include: *Inquisitions with Derek Jacobi, Impact Earth* (Channel 5); *Dalziel & Pascoe* (two series, BBC). Radio credits include: the award-winning *The Blood Libel, Eight Days in July, The Look of Life* (BBC Radio 4); a weekly current-affairs programme for BBC Radio 4 – *The Report*; the theme and music for *The Greek Who Stole Christmas* by Antony Horovitz, on audiobook. For more information about Simon's music go to www.slatermusic.com.

Clive Meldrum (Sound Designer)
Clive is Deputy Head of Sound at Birmingham Repertory Theatre.

Julia Horan (Casting Director)
Theatre credits include: *Annie Get Your Gun, Measure for Measure, Six Characters in Search of an Author, The House of Special Purpose, Bedroom Farce, Arcadia, When the Rain Stops Falling, The Hounding of David Oluwale, The Horse Marines, Edward Gant's Amazing Feats of Loneliness, Harvest, Drowning on Dry Land, In the Red and Brown Water, In a Dark Dark House, Nocturne, The Good Soul of Szechuan, Lost Highway, A Chain Plau, Kafka's Dick, The Homecoming, 3 Sisters on Hope Street, The Grouch, Swimming with Sharks, TinTin, Awake and Sing!, Absolute Beginners, Out of the Fog, We that are Left, Dying for It, Heartbreak House, Bad Jazz, The Soldier's Fortune, pool (no water), Gaddafi – A Living Myth, Rabbit, The Prayer Room, A Brief History of Helen of Troy, As You Like It, A Raisin in the Sun, The Morris, Port Authority, One Under, Sleeping Beauty, Anna in the Tropics, The Kindness of Strangers, Urban Legend, Yellowman, The Skin of our Teeth, Direct Action, Othello, Hobson's Choice, The Daughter-in-Law, Homebody/Kabul, The Girl on the Sofa,* Jerwood Young Directors Awards 2001 and 2004, *Original Sin, Les Liaisons Dangereuse, Antarctica, Action, My Brilliant Divorce, Yardgal, The Weir, The Force of Change, Holy Mothers, Last Dance at Dum Dum, Local, Made of Stone, About the Boy, Trade,* Playwrights in Schools Festival, Young Writers Festival 1998 and 2000, *Kindertransport.* Television includes: *Adha Cup, Parliamo Glasgow, Harvest, The Verdict, The Bill, The Badness of George IV.* Short films include: *Tea, Queen's Park Story.* Commercials include: *Utterly Butterly, Bendicks, AA, Psychosis.* Workshops and readings include: *All About My Mother, Marine Parade.*

Birmingham Repertory Theatre Company

Marketing Assistant
Donna Hounsell

Development Manager
Anya Sampson

Development Officer
Ros Adams

Theatre Manager
Nigel Cairns

Duty Managers
Darren Perry
Nicola Potocka

Sales Manager
Gerard Swift

Sales Team Supervisor
Rebecca Thorndyke

Sales Development Supervisor
Rachel Foster

Sales Team
Anne Bower
Kayleigh Cottam
Sebastian Maynard-Frances
Eileen Minnock
Jonathan Smith
Ryan Wootton

Senior Usher
Brenda Bradley

Thanks to our team of casual Box
Office staff, ushers and firemen

Stage Door Reception
Tracey Dolby
Robert Flynn
Neil Hill
Julie Plumb

Building Services Officer
Colin Williamson

Building Services Assistant
John Usowicz

Cleaning by We Clean Limited

Head Of Production
Tomas Wright

Production Manager
Milorad Zakula

Production Assistant
Hayley Seddon

Head Of Stage
Adrian Bradley

Deputy Head Of Stage
Kevin Smith

Stage Technicians
Mario Fortuin
Rosie Williams

Head Of Lighting
Andrew Fidgeon

Deputy Head Of Lighting
Phil Swoffer

Lighting Technicians
Anthony Aston
Simon Bond

Head Of Sound
Dan Hoole

Deputy Head Of Sound
Clive Meldrum

Company Manager
Ruth Morgan

Workshop Supervisor
Margaret Rees

Construction Co-ordinator
Oliver Shapley

Deputy Workshop Supervisor
Simon Fox

Head Scenic Artist
Christopher Tait

Properties And Armourer
Alan Bennett

Head Of Wardrobe
Sue Nightingale

Wardrobe Assistants
Lara Bradbeer
Melanie Francis
Brenda Huxtable
Debbie Williams

Head Of Wigs & Make-up
Andrew Whiteoak

**With thanks to the following
volunteers**
Student REPresentatives

REP Archivist
Horace Gillis

ᵀᴴᴱREP

Birmingham Repertory Theatre

Birmingham Repertory Theatre is one of Britain's leading national producing theatre companies. From its base in Birmingham, The REP produces over twenty new productions each year.

Artistic Director Rachel Kavanaugh's season of work for 2010 includes the world premieres of *Arthur & George*, adapted for the stage by David Edgar from Julian Barnes' novel, this production of Samantha Ellis's *Cling To Me Like Ivy* plus the UK premiere of Lutz Hübner's *Respect*. 2010 will also see brand-new productions of Brian Friel's *Dancing at Lughnasa* and Michael Frayn's *Noises Off*.

The commissioning and production of new work lies at the core of The REP's programme. The Door was established twelve years ago as a theatre dedicated to the production and presentation of new writing. In this time, it has given world premieres to new plays from a new generation of British playwrights. The Door aimed to provide a distinct alternative to the work seen in the Main House: a space where new voices and contemporary stories could be heard, that sought to create new audiences for the work of the company in this city and beyond. The Door has been a place to explore new ideas and different approaches to making theatre, to develop new plays and support emerging companies and artists.

Developing new and particularly younger audiences is also at the heart of The REP's work. The theatre's Learning and Participation department engage with over 10,000 young people each year through its various initiatives, including The Young REP, REP's Children, Grass Routes writing programme for 18–30 year olds, and the Transmissions young writers' programme. Transmissions has worked with hundreds of writers aged 12–25 across the region and the theatre's Playwriting Officer delivers programmes in schools to help establish playwriting in the National Curriculum. Grass Routes is for young artists aged 18–30 wishing to explore different ways of telling stories on stage, from playwriting to spoken word to grime theatre.

The REP's productions regularly transfer to London and tour nationally and internationally. Tours during 2009 included a new staging of Philip Pullman's *His Dark Materials*, Dennis Kelly's *Orphans*, Simon Stephens' *Pornography*, Charlie Dark's *Have Box Will Travel*, *Looking for Yoghurt* (a new play for young children which played at theatres in the UK, Japan and Korea) and *These Four Streets*, a multi-authored play about the 2005 Lozells disturbances.

In 2009, our production of *The Snowman* made its international debut at the Seoul Opera House, Korea, before returning to the UK for a 12th Christmas season at London's Peacock Theatre and a January run at The REP. Plans are underway for the show to travel further afield during 2010.

2010–2013 will be a significant period of development in the history of Birmingham Repertory Theatre as it integrates with the new £193 million Library of Birmingham, which will be built adjacent to the theatre. This development opportunity will allow the theatre to make many improvements to its current building as well as sharing a new 300-seat flexible studio theatre with the Library of Birmingham. The period will bring an exciting time artistically as audiences will be able to enjoy and experience an imaginative programme of REP productions in other theatres and non-theatrical spaces across Birmingham.

The Library of Birmingham project has also enabled The REP to rethink its new-writing policy, and with the intended third space, The Door will no longer be the only venue for the development and production of new work. This brings with it more opportunities to develop new writing and to consolidate the new work that already happens outside of The Door. The diversity of this new-writing work includes early years' work, new plays for The Young REP, the theatre's resident youth theatre, adaptations, responding to specific briefs, community plays, writer/performer collaborative writing, site-specific work and incorporating digital technology into the development and production of work. In addition to the commissioning of this work, The REP runs a writers' attachment programme aimed at enabling playwrights to experiment with new forms. In collaboration with the BME Theatre Initiative, supported by Arts Council, England (West Midlands), The REP aims to constantly explore the role of the writer and the form of telling stories in theatre.

Artistic Director Rachel Kavanaugh
Executive Director Stuart Rogers

Box Office: 0121 236 4455
Administration: 0121 245 2000
www.birmingham-rep.co.uk

Birmingham Repertory Theatre is a registered charity, number 223660

Supported by
**ARTS COUNCIL
ENGLAND**

CLING TO ME LIKE IVY

Samantha Ellis

For my family

Contents

Introduction

In May 2004, when 'Sheitel-gate' began, I was working part time in Joseph's Bookstore in Temple Fortune in North London. It started with a rumour that many of the *sheitels* – the wigs worn by married Orthodox Jewish women – might contravene Jewish law. A London-based rabbi had discovered that the hair for these wigs came from a Hindu temple in India, and since Orthodox Judaism considers Hinduism to involve idol worship – which would make the wigs questionable in Jewish law – he had gone on a fact-finding mission to the Tirupati Temple in Andhra Pradesh. From there he went to Jerusalem to make a decision that would affect Jewish women all over the world. And in the meantime, no one knew what to do. I saw women wearing rubber swimming caps, or synthetic fright wigs. There were bonfires of wigs on the streets of London, Jerusalem and New York. The *New York Times* called it 'an emotional upheaval within [the] Orthodox Jewish community' and that's how it felt to me. The bookshop was full of women wanting to discuss it, and the debates were fierce and passionate. A lot of the press coverage excluded the women's voices but it was the women who interested me – not just the Jewish women covering their hair from their wedding nights onwards, but the Hindu women who tipped their heads forward for a barber to shave them with a few deft strokes of a straight-edge blade, fulfilling pledges that if their rice crop was successful, perhaps, or if their child recovered from typhoid, they would sacrifice their beauty. I read that at the train station in Tirupati, you could tell who was arriving and who was leaving because the women who were leaving were all bald. And their hair might travel right across the world to a woman in Temple Fortune, a bride perhaps, nervous and excited about getting her first *sheitel*. The hair seemed like a communication between these two women – and after all they were both doing it (the shaving and the covering) for their faith.

I knew I wanted to turn this into a play when I read that Victoria Beckham had inadvertently sparked the whole crisis.

Asked if her hair extensions came from Russian prisoners forced to shave their heads, she'd joked that she had half Russian Cell Block H on her head. In the resulting fuss (inevitably called 'Extension-gate') it emerged that vast quantities of hair in the international hair trade came from the Tirupati Temple, which auctioned off four hundred tons of hair a year. I loved the idea that Posh Spice had unwittingly created havoc – and that she'd also enabled the Jewish community to start talking about hair covering in a really liberated way. And I couldn't resist the image of an Orthodox rabbi reading *OK!* magazine.

This was the first big crisis in Jewish law to play itself out online. For two heady weeks, Jewish blogs and web forums went wild. It felt like everything was being questioned, and it seemed possible that the laws on head covering might radically change. When a total ban on human-hair wigs was announced, many communities found this too stringent, and made their own decisions. I wanted to write about how diverse Jewish law is, how fabulously contrary.

The best thing about writing this play was feeling that I was connecting to another long history – of Jewish storytelling. All the Jews I know are full of stories. One of my earliest memories is of sitting under the kitchen table, aged four, pulling the leaves off parsley stalks for tabbouleh, while the grown-ups told stories above my head. I know Baghdad, where my family is from, entirely through stories. I know who I am because of those stories. One of the books I picked up at Joseph's was Avivah Gottlieb Zornberg's *The Beginning of Desire*. I had always thought the Talmud was a book of men arguing about the law, but Zornberg made me realise it was also full of stories. I love that the sages sat around like Hollywood screenwriters, looking at the stories that didn't quite make sense to them, filling in the gaps – a bit of backstory here, a new character there. They even wrote dialogue. The play's title comes from a *midrash* on the Book of Ruth. It's Boaz's chat-up line to Ruth, as imagined by Rashi. It's a much better line than anything I've ever made up.

Samantha Ellis

Thanks

Thank you to Shona Kundu, Lucy Michaels, Phil Pritchard, Dov Stekel, Chitra Sundaram, Andy Whiteoak and all at Gali Wigs for helping with the research for this play. Thank you to Caroline Jester for supporting the play from the seed of the idea, to Robert Anasi, Robin Booth, Stephen Brown, Gordon Haber, Paul King, Dominic Leggett, Matthew Morrison and Ben Musgrave for reading drafts and saying useful things, to Clare Lizzimore for directing an early reading, and to all the actors who read the play. Thank you to Nick Quinn for steadfast support, Emma Ayech for pop-culture expertise, and friendship, to Miranda Cook for cheerleading, to Naomi Alderman for stiffening my spine, to the MacDowell Colony where I wrote the first draft, and to all at Joseph's Bookstore where I had the idea. And a huge thank you to Sarah Esdaile for bringing it to the stage.

The writing of this play was supported by a grant from the European Association of Jewish Culture.

Characters

SHMULEY (*short for Shmuel*), *fifties, is an Orthodox Jewish rabbi, and a widower*

RIVKA, *twenty-one, is Shmuley's daughter, a nursery-school teacher*

DAVID, *twenty-three, is Rivka's fiancé, an optician*

MALKA, *seventies, is Rivka's maternal grandmother, born in Whitechapel, the daughter of Russian immigrants*

LEELA (*short for Leelavathi*), *twenty-one, is Rivka's best friend, a medical student, a Hindu who was born in India and emigrated when she was five*

PATRICK, *twenty-five, is a tree-sitter*

The actors playing David and Shmuley also play security guards

Setting

The play is set partly in the kitchen of Shmuley's house in North London, and partly in a wood in Hertfordshire, in the spring of 2004.

This text went to press before the end of rehearsals and so may differ slightly from the play as performed.

ACT ONE

Scene One

A Sunday afternoon in May 2004. SHMULEY's *kitchen in North London. A door leads to a hallway, where the telephone is, and also to the front door and the rest of the house. The kitchen is tatty but spotless, with two sinks and colour-coded crockery and cutlery. A Jewish festivals calendar hangs on the wall. A huge saucepan of soup is bubbling on the hob. Sun is coming through the window, shining on* RIVKA, *who is standing on a wooden chair in her wedding dress and socks, her arms up; occasionally she nervously touches her hair. There is something odd about it, though we don't yet know what. The dress is long-sleeved, high-necked, white and austere, but beautiful.* MALKA, *her mouth full of pins, is pinning it to take it in.* LEELA *sits at the table, with* OK! *magazine open in front of her.*

LEELA. Cos skinny women don't have daughters. Look at Victoria Beckham. She's got Romeo, but where's her Juliet? She's got Brooklyn but where's her...?

RIVKA. Chelsea?

LEELA. Yeah. If you're too thin your body thinks there's going to be hard times so you get boys. To work the fields and stuff.

MALKA. Did you get this from your doctor class or *OK!* magazine?

RIVKA. When's Victoria Beckham got hard times?

MALKA. Well, what's-his-face is having an affair.

RIVKA. Is he?

LEELA. Where have you been, Riv? Underwater?

RIVKA. Who's he having an affair with?

MALKA (*sniffing the dress*). Does it smell like mothballs still?

RIVKA. Not that Page Three Girl again?

LEELA (*sniffing the dress*). No.

MALKA. He had an affair already and she didn't divorce him? I suppose you can't blame him. What's-his-face. He probably just wants a *zaftig* girl, some flesh to squeeze.

LEELA. She's put on weight; they don't call her Skeletal Spice any more.

MALKA. She's still a *ferkrimpter*.

RIVKA (*automatically translating*). Sour-face.

LEELA. She doesn't smile cos she hates her dimples.

MALKA. Is it tight? We want you to be able to dance.

RIVKA. It's perfect.

MALKA. Your grandfather would roll in his grave if he saw me doing this. He was the best tailor on Princelet Street. His stitches were so tiny! He said I sewed like a bear. Okay, put down your arms.

RIVKA. Okay?

MALKA. Like a dream you look, *kayn eynhoreh*.

A moment where she looks at RIVKA. *They hear the front door opening and* MALKA *hides the magazine.* SHMULEY *enters, touching the* mezuzah *and kissing his fingers. He sees* RIVKA *and his eyes fill with tears.*

SHMULEY. Rivkele. You're changing your mother's dress?

MALKA. Who's changing it? We're altering it.

RIVKA (*getting down*). We just had to take it in, Dad.

MALKA. She's skinny like a noodle.

LEELA. But you're going to have grandsons.

SHMULEY. Grandsons?

MALKA (*to* LEELA). Sshh! (*To* SHMULEY.) One day, please God. And also granddaughters.

SHMULEY. I didn't know you were changing her dress.

RIVKA. It'll look the same, I promise, just the same.

SHMULEY (*wipes his eyes and makes an effort to smile*). You look very nice.

RIVKA. 'Nice'?

SHMULEY. You should always tell the bride she's beautiful. Even if she isn't beautiful! You can lie through your teeth and not only God won't mind, He even counts it a *mitzvah*! That's what Hillel says!

RIVKA. What does Shamai say?

SHMULEY. He disagrees.

RIVKA (*to* LEELA). He always disagrees.

SHMULEY. He says, 'What if the bride's blind or lame, disfigured, how can you lie and say she's beautiful?'

LEELA. Blind or lame?

SHMULEY. What, it's not politically correct?

LEELA (*laughs*). No!

RIVKA. It's the Middle Ages.

SHMULEY. Hillel wins though.

RIVKA. Hillel always wins.

SHMULEY. He says it doesn't matter what she looks like; make her happy. Hillel wasn't only a great sage, you know; he invented the sandwich.

SHMULEY *shuffles off, looking for something.*

RIVKA. So, do I look nice or are you lying?

MALKA. Who's lying? You look beautiful.

MALKA *hands* SHMULEY *his glasses, which he's been looking for. He exits.* RIVKA *touches her hair, as if she is surprised to find it on her head. She turns to* LEELA.

RIVKA. Okay, be honest.

LEELA. I've got to get used to you with straight hair.

RIVKA. Me too! It keeps getting in my face. It's in my eyes, my mouth.

LEELA. Yeah, but now you can do the flick.

LEELA *flicks her hair in a send-up of a sexy flick.*

RIVKA (*thrilled*). I know! (*Flicks.*) Like the Timotei advert.

She takes off what turns out to be a wig, to reveal her hair underneath. Where the wig was stiff and sleek, her hair is unruly. MALKA *takes the wig and pins it to a styrofoam head. She strokes it into shape.*

MALKA. So nice they make them now. You should have seen my first wig. My mother-in-law brought it from Russia. I put it on, I started itching. Everyone wanted to dance with the bride; I was too busy scratching my head. As soon as we got home, I ripped it off. My husband thought I was mad with desire; I just wanted to look at it. And what was in there? Insects! Crawling things! I told him: there are things moving in this *sheitel* and I want a new one. The complaining he did! The sighing! You'd have thought I asked for a divorce.

RIVKA *and* LEELA *laugh.* SHMULEY *enters.*

Take the dress off. Careful of the pins.

LEELA. I'll help you.

RIVKA *and* LEELA *exit.* MALKA *goes towards the pan on the hob.*

MALKA. There's soup. Don't argue!

SHMULEY. I'll be late for the *shul* committee.

She starts making him a sandwich instead.

MALKA. How can you work on air? Don't forget to say about that leak. In the women's section? Three weeks now we're sitting round a bucket. Last *Shabbes* it was dripping right through the *amidah*. And who knows what it's doing to the roof? If it was in the men's section, they'd find the money.

SHMULEY. If it was in the men's section, Alan Baum would be up a ladder himself.

MALKA (*laughs*). That *noodnik*.

SHMULEY. I thought you said he was handsome?

MALKA. He's not handsome; he's a fruitarian. (*Pause. She looks at him.*) It was a shock for you, seeing her in that dress.

SHMULEY. Like walking into my own wedding.

MALKA. You cried then too.

SHMULEY. I couldn't believe my luck, to get a girl like Sarah.

MALKA. That suit needs dry cleaning.

SHMULEY. Does it?

MALKA. Yes!

She brushes off some lint, vigorously. He laughs and moves away.

SHMULEY. I'm not your son; I only married your daughter. (*Sighs.*) I wish she was here.

MALKA. You don't think I wish that?

SHMULEY. Every morning, I wake up and I forget. I reach across the bed then I remember.

RIVKA and LEELA enter; RIVKA is now wearing a shapeless long skirt and a long-sleeved shirt buttoned to the top. She immediately puts the kettle on, gets out a large saucepan and starts making carrot tzimmes.

RIVKA. Dad, did you check when Mrs Horowitz is coming for dinner?

SHMULEY. Maybe tonight, maybe tomorrow.

RIVKA. You didn't check?

SHMULEY. Does it make such a difference?

MALKA. She's *broigus* with the Katzes. They're coming tomorrow.

SHMULEY. Since when's she *broigus* with the Katzes?

MALKA. Five, six years already. They had an argument about a cut-glass bowl.

SHMULEY (*laughs*). Okay: a man goes to his rabbi, holding a beigel. He says, 'Rabbi, why does all our bread have holes in?' The rabbi tells him,' It's not that our bread has holes in; it's that our holes have bread *around* them.' It's the glass-half-full, but Jewish! It's good, no? Maybe I'll tell the Katzes. Life's too short to argue over cut glass.

MALKA. Maybe it was crystal.

RIVKA. Dad, I was confirming the flowers for the *mechitza* and Mrs Fishbein says it's three inches too short. I ordered it the height we always get them.

MALKA. Yes, but if she talks…

RIVKA. She won't talk if Dad says it's okay. She can't fight the rabbi.

MALKA. That woman can fight anyone.

RIVKA. But the height's okay, isn't it?

SHMULEY. I don't know now, Rivka. I'll be late.

RIVKA. But I have to tell the florist, Dad. They have to build the frame, and order flowers –

SHMULEY. So make it higher.

MALKA. Because Mrs Fishbein says so? You're the rabbi.

RIVKA. She says if the men jump, they can see the women.

MALKA. Who's jumping?

RIVKA. When they dance. (*To* SHMULEY, *who is sidling towards the door.*) Dad!

SHMULEY. Make it higher, Rivka. It's better to be on the safe side.

Little pause. RIVKA *and* MALKA *are both deflated.*

MALKA. Maybe you're right. Then no one has any reason to say anything against us. Here.

She gives SHMULEY *the sandwich but he doesn't take it.*

SHMULEY. I'll eat later.

MALKA. At least take an apple!

She seizes an apple, wipes it on her cardigan and holds it out to him. He takes it and exits.

Rivka, do you want a sandwich?

RIVKA. I have to call the florist.

She exits. MALKA *turns to* LEELA.

MALKA. Do you want it?

LEELA. No, thanks.

MALKA. Nobody eats any more.

She puts the sandwich in the fridge. She gets out OK! *magazine.*

And why does this *meeskeit* have a problem with dimples? When I got married I had dimples, I had hips!

LEELA. Did your husband like that?

MALKA. Who knows what he liked? He was a *nebbish*.

LEELA. I thought he was the best tailor on Princelet Street.

MALKA (*ominously*). Never marry a man with small hands.

RIVKA enters.

RIVKA. She's doing it *four* inches higher. 'To be on the safe side.'

MALKA *kisses the top of her head. She exits.* RIVKA *pushes back her sleeves and unbuttons the top button of her shirt. She goes back to cooking.* LEELA *gets out a compact mirror and starts doing her face.*

LEELA. Riv, if my mum calls, I'm staying over tonight, okay?

RIVKA. Where are you going?

LEELA. Up Patrick's tree!

RIVKA. You're not.

LEELA. I so am!

RIVKA. But what if it rains?

LEELA. He says it's warm. He says it's magical, he says the tree houses are like birds' nests.

RIVKA. 'Magical'?

LEELA (*laughs*). I know! A load of yogurt-weaving crusties up a tree with no hot water; where's the magic? I told him: 'If the chainsaws come, I'm out of there. I'm not fighting for a tree.' Oh, Riv: Mum thinks I'm staying Tuesday too. Got to use my alibi while I can.

RIVKA. I can still be your alibi when I'm married.

LEELA. Not three nights a week you can't. Mum won't buy it. She's already suspicious. (*Sighs.*) She'll be wrecked when she finds out.

RIVKA. But why does she have to find out? You never told her about Tony.

LEELA. Tony! Course not.

RIVKA. Or Paul.

LEELA. Paul! I think I love Patrick. Like, this is it. I feel like I'm being torn apart.

RIVKA. Did you tell him that?

LEELA. You don't say it first and give them all the power.

RIVKA. I told David first.

LEELA. Yeah, but you and David...

RIVKA. What?

LEELA. It's different.

RIVKA. No it's not. Why's it different?

LEELA. You've never even snogged him.

RIVKA. Yeah, but –

LEELA. Patrick can't keep his hands off me.

RIVKA. Sex isn't everything.

LEELA. You sound like something out of your brides' class.
Hey, have you asked them if he's allowed to go down on you
when you're married?

RIVKA. David will know.

LEELA. He blatantly won't.

RIVKA. Why are you being like this about David?

LEELA. What are you being like about Patrick?

RIVKA. I've never met him. It's been three months! You're
supposed to be my best friend.

LEELA. I didn't know if it would be okay to bring him round.

RIVKA. Of course it would be okay! It's like you're
embarrassed.

LEELA. Course I'm not.

RIVKA. Like I'm not cool enough.

LEELA. I'll introduce you.

RIVKA. I don't have time. The wedding! And school. The
children know I'm stressed, and they keep playing up. And I
told Dad to stop inviting people over every night, but –

LEELA. Riv… stop doing that.

RIVKA. Sorry.

LEELA. Sit down.

RIVKA (*an outburst*). Is it going to hurt?

LEELA. Riv…?

RIVKA. They said it might hurt and we're supposed to breathe.
And take some paracetamol.

LEELA. That's just cruel! It isn't going to hurt. You do *want* to shag David, right? (*Beat.*) What do you feel when you, like, brush against his arm or something? Like, do you get a sort of charge? Like a shiver.

RIVKA. But I've never.

LEELA. You must've. Accidentally. Just to see.

RIVKA. It wouldn't be an accident if it was to see.

LEELA. You could, you know. It's easy. You could just brush against him. Just like that.

She brushes against RIVKA*'s arm.*

RIVKA. But what if I don't feel anything? We're getting married.

Pause. Then LEELA *has an idea.*

LEELA. I could get you a vibrator!

RIVKA. No – Leela –

LEELA. They do really small ones, you could get used to the idea –

RIVKA (*covering her face*). I'd be too embarrassed.

LEELA. Riv –

RIVKA. I don't want to talk about it.

LEELA. Yeah, but –

RIVKA. I can't, okay? I can't! (*Little pause.*) Sorry.

LEELA. Don't be sorry. (*Little pause.*) I know it's your religion, I know it's what you want, but I just can't get my head around it.

RIVKA. I know.

LEELA. David's a sweetheart. I'm sure he'll be lovely.

RIVKA. Yeah.

LEELA. We could talk if you want. Ask me anything.

RIVKA. It's okay.

LEELA. Well, any time.

RIVKA. Okay. Thanks.

LEELA. Okay.

RIVKA. Can I really meet Patrick?

LEELA. You'll hate him.

RIVKA. I won't.

LEELA. He isn't *nice*. My mum would be disgusted.

RIVKA. That's just cos he's not a Hindu.

LEELA gets a text message.

LEELA. And cos he's an anarchist, he lives up a tree. (*Looking at the text, she erupts.*) Shit!

RIVKA. What?

LEELA. 'Sorry, babe, tonight's off'? And, 'Have a good one'? Half an hour's notice. I could be freezing my tits off waiting for him. I've got all dressed up, like a twat.

She starts texting.

RIVKA. Don't text him back.

LEELA. I bet he's shagging Tinkerbell.

RIVKA. 'Tinkerbell'?

LEELA. They all have names like that. She's twenty-eight and dresses like she's seven: pink and glitter. Crop tops. (*She presses 'send' on her phone.*) He'd better reply.

The doorbell rings. RIVKA puts away the magazine, rebuttons her blouse and pushes her sleeves down.

RIVKA. That's David. Stay. Stay and have dinner.

She exits. LEELA rushes after her and almost bumps into DAVID. He steps back to avoid touching her.

LEELA. I'm sorry!

She exits as RIVKA *is coming back in.*

RIVKA. Just a sec.

RIVKA *exits.* DAVID *touches the* mezuzah *and kisses his fingers. He takes off his coat. He sees the wig. Checking no one's there, he reaches out to touch it. He strokes it. He hears a noise, jumps, and moves away.* MALKA *enters.*

MALKA. David! How are you keeping?

DAVID. I'm fine, and you?

MALKA (*looking into the pan, adjusting the heat*). Busy! You know… The family's fine?

DAVID. They send their love.

She moves the wig to a less conspicuous place.

MALKA. That *rugelach* your sister sent was lovely. Tell her thank you.

She starts emptying the washing machine as RIVKA *enters.*

RIVKA. Sorry: Leela's having boyfriend trouble. I'll do that.

MALKA. What am I, a hundred and five?

RIVKA (*putting the kettle on*). Do you want some tea?

DAVID. If you're making.

MALKA. Not for me.

MALKA *exits with a basket of laundry.*

DAVID. How does he wash, Leela's boyfriend, living up a tree?

RIVKA. When I meet him, I'll ask him. She's going to bring him round before the wedding.

Getting out a bowl, she starts shaping beaten eggs and matzoh meal into kneidlach *and dropping them into the pan.*

DAVID. Only two more weeks! I can't wait.

RIVKA (*nervous*). Yeah.

The kettle has boiled. She makes him a cup of tea and brings it over.

DAVID. Thanks.

He murmurs a blessing. He sips a bit of tea. A slightly awkward silence and then he starts, flirtatiously.

I was studying this *midrash* on the Book of Ruth. There's this bit, at the end of the story. You know when Naomi's trying to get Ruth and Boaz together? She tells Ruth to go to a party, but to go late, when Boaz will have passed out drunk. And she's got to uncover his feet. You know when they say 'feet', it doesn't mean *feet*, you know some people say it's a metaphor, some people say it's a *euphemism*, in this case the rabbis don't agree, but –

RIVKA. I know what it means!

DAVID. Sorry. I embarrassed you.

RIVKA. It's fine!

DAVID. So it works: they get married, they live happily ever after. But the rabbis thought there was something missing. In the story. So they add this bit. They actually put words in Ruth and Boaz's mouths. So Boaz wakes up, it's dark, there's Ruth, he's... uncovered, and he asks, 'Are you a spirit or a woman?' And he touches her head and says, 'You must be a woman, cos spirits don't have hair.'

RIVKA. How come?

DAVID. It doesn't say. So then he asks her, 'Are you married or single?' She says, 'Single.' 'Are you clean or unclean?' 'Clean.' And he says, 'Who are you?' And she says, 'You're my saviour.' And he says, 'Cling to me like ivy and I'll be with you all my life.'

RIVKA. But she's just this stranger in the dark. He doesn't know it's her.

DAVID. That's what's so great about it. No matter what happens, he's committing; so long as she clings to him, he's there. It's like: marriage is a risk, you know? A leap of faith.

RIVKA. Not if you marry someone you actually know.

DAVID. You might know them now but you don't know what they're going to be like in five years or ten. People change. I thought you'd like it: 'Cling to me like ivy.'

RIVKA. Ivy strangles trees. And buildings. Rips the bricks apart.

DAVID (*excited*). I didn't think of that. The sages, they never mention that.

RIVKA. When Boaz says it to her, have they slept together?

DAVID. Well, one text says she seizes him and he gets hard like a... like an uncooked turnip.

RIVKA. Really?

DAVID. Yeah, those sages.

RIVKA. Maybe that's why he commits. If they've slept together. Because he knows it's going to be okay. I don't mean if you haven't then you can't, just... (*She panics.*)

DAVID. It's going to be okay, Rivka. I love you. Since my *Bar Mitzvah*. I couldn't reach the *bimah*. You brought that apple crate for me to stand on.

RIVKA. You winked at me.

DAVID. I know! With the Torah scroll in my hands!

RIVKA *laughs*. SHMULEY *enters, hurriedly touching the* mezuzah *and kissing his fingers.*

SHMULEY. Malka? Rivka? Have you heard of someone called Victoria Beckton?

RIVKA. Why?

SHMULEY. She's giving me a lot of problems!

MALKA *enters.*

MALKA. What problems can Victoria Beckham give you?

SHMULEY. She said something on TV. And now they're saying there's a problem with the *sheitels*. Rivka, where's yours from?

RIVKA. Limor of London.

SHMULEY. No, not the wig; the hair.

RIVKA. The hair?

SHMULEY. They didn't tell you where it comes from? Call and ask: 'Is it from India?' They're saying it's *avodah zara*. Go! Call and ask!

RIVKA *exits*.

DAVID. How can a wig be idol worship?

SHMULEY. There's a temple in India. The women sacrifice their hair to a big golden idol and this is the hair they're bringing to put on our women's heads!

MALKA. What about my *sheitel*? And Mrs Horowitz covers her head – she'll want to know.

RIVKA *enters*.

RIVKA. Does this mean I can't wear it at the wedding?

SHMULEY. Is it from India?

RIVKA. There's no answer on her phone.

MALKA. It's probably ringing off the hook.

RIVKA. If it's from India then I can't wear it? Dad?

SHMULEY. Rabbi Dunner's gone to India –

MALKA. From St John's Wood? What does he want in India?

SHMULEY. It's a fact-finding mission, and then he'll go to make the decision in Jerusalem.

RIVKA. But the wedding's in two weeks!

SHMULEY. I don't know if we should even have that *sheitel* in the house!

The phone starts ringing.

Don't answer that! I need time to think.

MALKA. But people are going to want your advice, Shmuley! You're the rabbi.

SHMULEY. I wish this Victoria Spice had kept her mouth shut.

MALKA. Shmuley, you're confused; she's nothing to do with us. She's not even Jewish.

DAVID. But David Beckham might be.

RIVKA. Really?

DAVID. Only his grandfather – halachically he's out.

RIVKA (*excited*). But still.

MALKA. But what does she know from *sheitels*?

SHMULEY. I don't know! She said something on TV!

MALKA. If you rabbis read the Talmud instead of watching TV we wouldn't have this problem. You're not supposed to know who Victoria Beckham is.

DAVID. You can't live in this world and not know who Victoria Beckham is.

SHMULEY. So now everyone knows who she is!

RIVKA (*crying*). I wanted it to be a perfect wedding...

MALKA. Oh, Rivka, Rivkele...

She goes to comfort her. Lights down.

Scene Two

Three days later, early evening. The kitchen. LEELA, RIVKA
and PATRICK. *He is in combat trousers and an oversized,
ragged fisherman's jumper. He is eating soup. Something is
cooking in the oven.* RIVKA *is wrapping sugared almonds in
coloured paper and ribbons.* LEELA *intermittently helps but is
also flicking through* OK!

LEELA. Even *OK!* magazine's turned against her now.

RIVKA. They're so fickle.

LEELA. She's not a doormat like they're saying; she's just
    practical. You don't dump David Beckham, do you?

RIVKA. But do you think she's forgiven him?

LEELA. No, I bet she's giving him hell behind closed doors.
    He'll feel so guilty, she'll have him wrapped around her little
    finger.

PATRICK. Would you forgive him?

RIVKA. Jews don't do forgiveness; we do guilt.

LEELA. I'd forgive him.

PATRICK. You fancy him; you have no objectivity.

LEELA. She says he's an animal in bed, that's all I'm saying.

PATRICK. That PA; she's fit.

LEELA. She's a slag.

PATRICK. Aren't you all piss and vinegar?

LEELA. You don't take another woman's man. Mates before
    muff.

PATRICK. Women can't say that.

LEELA. I'm reclaiming it.

PATRICK. Oh, now you're all about the sisterhood.

LEELA. I'm always all about the sisterhood. My mum got married off at fourteen and look at me, I'm going to be a doctor. One generation.

PATRICK. Look at you: one generation from hard graft on the land to lipgloss and Girl Power.

LEELA. Not Girl Power. It's depressing about the Spice Girls.

PATRICK. Because they're shit?

LEELA. No: because there's five strong, successful, mouthy women, men come on the scene and they fall apart.

RIVKA. We used to love them.

LEELA. Yeah: past tense.

RIVKA. We had routines to all their songs.

LEELA. We were twelve, Riv.

RIVKA. It's so stuffy in here.

PATRICK. This is so prurient; here's some picture of a jewel-encrusted whip he got her.

LEELA. Swarovski crystals, yeah.

PATRICK. Have you memorised this entire magazine?

LEELA. Why are you reading it? I thought you went up a tree to get away from this stuff.

PATRICK. Hey, did you tell Rivka about coming up?

LEELA. Yeah, in the pouring rain.

PATRICK. I should've made you shimmy up; then you'd know wet.

LEELA. The birds were screeching in my ears. The food was shit.

PATRICK. Leelavathi got all arsey cos the others had the nerve to make a curry –

LEELA. Mash with curry powder in's not curry.

RIVKA. What do you do in the tree house?

PATRICK. Eat, sleep, read. Make lock-on devices ready for evictions. Make music, make love...

LEELA *hits him.*

Hey! We did make love...

LEELA. It was the only way to get warm.

PATRICK. Give it a nice evening with a cool breeze, the branches creaking, and it smells all cool and dark and sticky, your feet don't touch ground in five days; you feel the sunshine, you feel the rain...

LEELA. Yeah, and then you get dragged out of a tree and go to prison.

RIVKA. Why do you do it?

PATRICK. I just think if I can save one tree with my body then why wouldn't I? Some people acquiesce, but I'm a fighter. I came out of the womb like this.

He holds up a fist in the air, like Superman in flight.

LEELA. You did not.

PATRICK. Ask my mum.

MALKA *enters with a tape measure.*

MALKA. Rivka, I need your arm.

LEELA. Malka, this is Patrick.

RIVKA *holds out her arm.* MALKA *takes a measurement.*

PATRICK. Oh, then this is your soup. It's gorgeous.

MALKA. Have more! There's plenty! One bowl and you can walk across Russia. The sugared almonds are lovely. Leela, take one for your mum; it's good luck.

LEELA. Thanks.

She takes a bundle of sugared almonds. MALKA *exits.*

RIVKA. Do you want some more?

PATRICK. I'm stuffed.

He takes the bowl over and puts it in one of the sinks.
RIVKA *rushes over in a panic.*

LEELA. You put it in the milk sink.

RIVKA *fills the kettle and puts it on. She puts tea towels on the floor.*

RIVKA. Sorry.

PATRICK. What did I do?

LEELA. That one's for meat and that's for milk. They have to keep them separate.

RIVKA *pours the whole kettle-full of boiling water into the sink and over the counter. She stands back, relieved, as the water runs down. She dries off the sink. She puts all the tea towels she has used into the washing machine.*

PATRICK. Like, completely separate?

RIVKA. Yeah, even the smell of them or the steam when it rises.

PATRICK. How do you keep the smell separate? The steam?

RIVKA. It's like there's these invisible lines everywhere. You don't cross them.

PATRICK. All these tiny details.

RIVKA. Everything matters, that's why. God's not in the sky; He's in your kitchen. And He cares which sink you use, what spoon.

PATRICK. I'd rather He stopped us destroying the earth. (*Laughs.*) Broken record, me.

RIVKA. I like that nothing's meaningless.

PATRICK. Oh, I get that.

RIVKA. Yeah?

PATRICK. You wouldn't get this 'Posh and Becks' crap if we made things meaningful.

RIVKA. But that's a marriage breaking up; it means something.

PATRICK. It's not a real marriage; it's just plastic, empty, for the cameras.

RIVKA. Maybe.

PATRICK. Anyway I don't believe in marriage, commitment, any of that.

RIVKA. Really?

PATRICK. If you chain love up, it dies.

LEELA has taken the wig off the styrofoam head and put it on. She flicks it.

LEELA. What do you think, is it me?

PATRICK. Bloody hell. What's that?

RIVKA. Leela!

PATRICK. Why've you got a wig?

RIVKA. You'll stretch the netting.

LEELA. Are you saying I've got a big head?

RIVKA. Don't...

LEELA. It's for after she gets married. This could be my hair, you know. Well, my mum's.

RIVKA. Please.

LEELA. Well, it could, right? Be my hair.

RIVKA. Take it off!

LEELA. All right!

She takes the wig off. She gives it to RIVKA *who puts it back on the styrofoam head.*

PATRICK. You're going to shave your head?

LEELA. She isn't going to *shave*! Jewish men don't want their wives all bald, do they?

RIVKA. Some women shave.

LEELA. Euughhh. Really?

PATRICK leans across and lifts the weight of RIVKA*'s hair in his hands.*

PATRICK. It's gorgeous hair you've got. It's a shame to hide it.

It's the first time RIVKA *has been touched by any man but her father. She's electrified. And, belatedly, she breaks away.*

LEELA. You're not supposed to touch her.

PATRICK. I'm sorry, Rivka.

LEELA. Do you have to pour boiling water over *him* now?

MALKA *calls: 'Rivka!' from the hallway.*

RIVKA. It's fine.

RIVKA *exits.* LEELA *goes to sit on* PATRICK*'s lap.*

PATRICK. So, you're not still pissed off about Sunday night?

LEELA. I am a bit.

PATRICK. Or maybe you just like being pissed off. The drama.

LEELA. I don't like getting stood up. I know you're Mr No-Commitment, but you should be able to commit to meeting up at least.

PATRICK. So why don't you tell your mum about me?

LEELA. What's that got to do with it?

PATRICK. Cos I'd like to see some commitment out of you. You're supposed to be an independent woman, a medic, all that; you call yourself a feminist and you can't tell your mum you've got a boyfriend.

LEELA. You're the one who's always saying you don't know when you're going to be up a tree, you're *in flux* –

PATRICK. Yeah, and you're mucking us up with secrets and lies.

LEELA. It's easy for you. I can't do what I want unless I lie.

PATRICK. Well, I'm a grown-up; I can't be doing with all this sneaking around.

RIVKA *enters*.

RIVKA. Sorry. The wedding dress...

PATRICK. We should make tracks, Leelavathi. Don't want to miss the film. Can I use your...?

RIVKA. It's just through there. The light's on the outside.

He goes. LEELA *immediately turns to her.*

LEELA. So...? Come on.

RIVKA. He's great.

LEELA. Really?

RIVKA. Yeah. (*Laughs.*) When you said he was an anarchist, I thought he'd be, like, rude.

LEELA. Riv!

RIVKA. He uses your whole name.

LEELA. Yeah, and his texts are full of semicolons. Did you see how sweet he was after he touched your hair? He blushed.

RIVKA. He was embarrassed. I feel bad –

LEELA. Some eco-warrior he is; he's marshmallow.

RIVKA. He's got nice eyes.

She stops herself, feeling she's said too much.

LEELA (*possessive*). Yeah, you should see him with his kit off.

LEELA laughs as PATRICK *enters.* RIVKA *turns away in embarrassment.*

PATRICK. My ears are burning.

LEELA. So vain.

PATRICK (*hoisting up his rucksack*). Well, it was grand to meet you.

RIVKA. You too. Good luck. Saving your tree.

PATRICK. You should come and see it. It's only down the Metropolitan line. (*To* LEELA.) Come on, you.

RIVKA. See you, Leela.

LEELA. Later.

PATRICK. Oh, and good luck.

RIVKA. For what?

PATRICK. For your wedding.

They exit. RIVKA *holds onto the table and takes a couple of deep breaths. She picks up her hair the way* PATRICK *did but then the phone rings and she jumps guiltily and drops her hair.* MALKA *answers the phone.* RIVKA *goes back to the almonds.* MALKA *enters.*

MALKA. Mrs Horowitz again. 'Any news?' she says. Like we wouldn't call if we had news? (*She opens the freezer and appraises its contents.*) You think we need to go to Kosher King?

RIVKA. Did I tell you what Mrs Fishbein was wearing today at school? A swimming cap. Her cousin the rabbi told her to.

MALKA (*shutting the freezer*). A rubber swimming cap?

RIVKA. With daisies on.

MALKA. Her cousin's enjoying this.

RIVKA. She wants all the teachers to do the same. I said, 'Well, I'm not married.' She said, 'You will be soon.' Like it was a threat.

The doorbell rings. Both MALKA *and* RIVKA *go for* OK! *magazine at the same time. They laugh.* RIVKA *hides the magazine and* MALKA *exits. By the time* MALKA *and* DAVID *enter, she has gone back to wrapping the sugared almonds. He touches the* mezuzah *and kisses his fingers.*

DAVID (*of the sugared almonds*). Oh, look at these!

MALKA. Rivka's been working all afternoon.

RIVKA. And Leela.

MALKA. *Nu*, David, is your dad also getting phone calls every five minutes?

DAVID. He's going crazy.

MALKA. This rabbi is having a holiday in India and we're all waiting.

DAVID. I heard he's out there, interviewing peasant women, illiterate – asking them theological questions.

RIVKA. You know, Leela went to Tirupati.

DAVID. Did she?

RIVKA. Yeah, she had typhoid and her mum made this pledge, if she got over it she'd sacrifice her hair –

MALKA. You know they're burning wigs in the street? In New York, in Jerusalem… And how does it make us look to the *goyim*?

DAVID. It isn't going to happen here; don't worry.

RIVKA. Why do we have to burn the wigs? If we can't use them then there's this cancer charity. Locks of Love.

DAVID (*sighs*). We can't. My dad said what if the wig ends up going to a Jewish patient? And you can't get pleasure from idol worship, and giving to charity is considered pleasure.

RIVKA. But if we could help people with cancer…

DAVID. I know.

MALKA. If we have to burn the wigs, we have to burn the wigs, but why does it have to be in the street? Why wash our dirty things in public? Rivka, if I call Schlagman's, do you think two chickens is enough?

RIVKA. Only two fit in the pot.

MALKA kisses RIVKA's head.

MALKA. What am I going to do without you?

She exits. Pause. RIVKA has barely been looking at DAVID. She screws up her eyes.

RIVKA. I've, um, I've got something in my eye. Can you see it?

DAVID. Push your hair back. Come into the light.

They move near to the window. She pushes back her hair.

Which eye is it?

RIVKA. Um. My, um, my left eye.

DAVID. I can't see anything. Maybe if I lifted your eyelid. (*Pause.*) It's allowed. For medical reasons. I can... touch you.

DAVID *hesitates.*

RIVKA. I'll do it myself. In the mirror.

She is about to go.

DAVID. No, just let me wash my hands.

RIVKA. Okay.

He washes his hands over-thoroughly.

DAVID. Is there a cloth?

RIVKA. There.

She nearly holds her breath with nervous excitement as he dries his hands.

DAVID. Okay. I need to lift your eyelid...

RIVKA. Okay.

DAVID. Okay.

He touches her eye. He's electrified.

I can't see anything. It might have gone. Blink.

RIVKA. It must have gone by itself.

She has felt nothing. She is horribly disappointed. She moves away.

DAVID. Rivka! You don't blink enough. Don't screw up your eyes. Just gently bring your lids together, then come apart. That's it. You've got enough tears. You're just not letting them out. You have to blink. The tears wash out the eyes.

Like windscreen wipers. (*Little pause*.) Is it... definitely gone? Are you okay?

RIVKA (*blinking back tears of disappointment*). It's gone. Yeah. It's fine.

Lights down.

Scene Three

A week later, evening. The kitchen. RIVKA is washing up. MALKA is drying. SHMULEY, DAVID and LEELA sit at the table with DAVID's laptop, a few heavy, leather-bound volumes of the Talmud and a copy of OK! magazine.

DAVID (*with the confidence of the expert*). So you don't get your hair cut near where the god is, not in the temple, not in the temple grounds, and the people who cut your hair aren't monks or sadhus or spiritual in any way?

LEELA (*impressed*). No. I mean yes. You're right.

DAVID. And they're not praying, you're not praying, no one's praying?

LEELA. It's a barber's shop.

DAVID. The barbers don't pray then? Not even under their breath? Before they cut your hair or after, nothing?

LEELA. It's quick. You tip your head forward, he's got a straight-edge blade, it's gone. (*To* RIVKA.) Can you believe I had typhoid? So medieval.

DAVID (*to* SHMULEY). Are you thinking what I'm thinking?

SHMULEY. Let's not get too excited – let's check the Steinsaltz.

DAVID. But if they're just barbers...

SHMULEY. I know! I know! Come.

SHMULEY *and* DAVID *exit.* LEELA *gets out a compact mirror and looks at a bruise on her mouth.*

LEELA. It's really obvious it's bruised.

RIVKA. Well, in the light…

LEELA. Mum's *so* going to notice!

RIVKA. I don't understand; did he *bite* you?

LEELA. He gets carried away. He's very passionate.

RIVKA *inadvertently touches her own lip but stops as* DAVID *and* SHMULEY *enter, each with another heavy book.*

SHMULEY. This is just like being at *yeshiva*; arguing about the law. Except, instead of your grandfather, we've got you.

DAVID. I've got less beard than him.

SHMULEY. It's amazing what he did; to go to the desert. Start a *yeshiva* out of nothing!

DAVID. It was a lot of pressure when I didn't want to be a rabbi.

He starts typing information into an online forum.

SHMULEY. I had the opposite from my parents. Imagine me, going round to them – they didn't even keep *Shabbes*, they went to *shul* three times a year, they parked around the corner and pretended they walked – imagine me going in a beard and saying, 'This is me now.'

LEELA. You were a rebel.

SHMULEY. You know what? I never cared about that stuff until the Six Day War. They were talking about throwing Jews in the sea. I was twenty-one, I was reckless, I got on a plane.

LEELA. You were going to fight?

SHMULEY. Well. I arrived on the fifth day – who knew it would be such a short war? I was too embarrassed to go home. I went to a kibbutz. They put me in the chicken house.

I met these people. I wanted to be like them, to know what I was doing, to know why. I'm still waiting!

DAVID. This is amazing. Jews, all over the world, sitting in their kitchens, trying to solve this – and now, with the internet, we can talk to each other. This blog's got five hundred and thirty-four comments!

SHMULEY. Yes, but who's commenting? They could be anyone. They could be women!

LEELA (*laughs*). Not women!

DAVID. This one says he's in Rio. Who knew there were Jews in Rio?

MALKA. If I only knew I could be a Jew in Rio…

DAVID. It's like the old days of the talmudic debates. Just people, trying to work out what God wants from us. This conversation's been going on a thousand years!

MALKA (*yawns*). Has it?

SHMULEY (*laughs*). Does it feel that long?

MALKA. Talk, fine, talk. But the decision's still going to be made by two men in Jerusalem.

DAVID. Maybe we won't listen to Jerusalem.

MALKA. You mean we could go our own way? Every rabbi does his own thing?

DAVID. Why not? We've studied Talmud, we've got brains; we can *solve* this!

SHMULEY (*gloomily leafing through* OK!). Why do they call this woman 'Posh Spice'? And what does 'bling' mean?

MALKA (*snatching the magazine*). Enough Victoria Beckham now! This isn't her fault!

SHMULEY. It's all her fault!

MALKA. How can this be her fault? She's a singer, Shmuley. She sings.

LEELA. 'Sings' is pushing it.

SHMULEY. If she sings or if she doesn't sing; she started this!

RIVKA. It's cos of that controversy about her hair extensions.

LEELA. Extension-gate!

RIVKA. Yeah, she got interviewed on TV and they said, 'How do you feel about wearing hair that probably got shaved off some prisoner in a Russian jail?' And she just laughed –

LEELA. And she said: 'I've got half Russian Cell Block H on my head!'

RIVKA. But then the next day they were saying it was icky, you know, all these women who get forced to shave their heads –

LEELA. And murderers and stuff; it *is* icky.

MALKA. So if the hair's from Russia, what's the problem?

SHMULEY. It's not from Russia!

MALKA. She just said Russian murderers!

RIVKA. Yeah, but the next day her publicists came out and said the hair's not from Russia, it's from India.

LEELA. They made it sound like we sacrificed our hair cos we *wanted* Victoria Beckham to have it. We didn't know they were auctioning it off. A pound a strand! I'm going to start scraping out the plughole. I'll never be skint again.

DAVID. Wait: you didn't even know they auctioned it off?

LEELA. The barber chucked it in a bin and that's the last we saw of it.

DAVID (*thrilled*). Really? In a bin? (*Types furiously.*)

LEELA. Yeah.

MALKA. You know what's going to happen? They're going to ban the wigs. Because they're so nice now. Before, we all looked the same; now, the girls look like supermodels!

DAVID (*still typing*). I've never been sure how I feel about covering hair with hair.

MALKA. You have to cover it with something.

DAVID. Maybe not. Maybe things could change.

SHMULEY (*laughs*). How many Orthodox rabbis does it take to change a light bulb? (*Little pause.*) Change? What change?

DAVID. Yes, but the word does have three meanings.

RIVKA. What word?

DAVID. *Parah*.

SHMULEY. A woman's accused of adultery but she says she didn't do it, so – this is a thousand years ago – the rabbi tests her. First he takes off her clothes –

LEELA. The rabbi does?

DAVID. It's supposed to be an echo, to remind her of the affair.

LEELA. *If* she had an affair.

Her mobile rings, she fishes for it in her bag.

DAVID. Yeah.

SHMULEY. The idea is, she'll get embarrassed, she might confess she's been unfaithful – problem solved.

RIVKA. Of course she'll get embarrassed – he's ripping off her clothes!

SHMULEY. No one said 'ripping', Rivka.

LEELA (*answering the phone*). Hi, babes…

She exits with the phone.

DAVID. The Rambam did. (*Showing him.*) Look how it changes over time. In Numbers, he's uncovering her hair. In the *Mishnah*, he's grabbing her clothes and if they tear, they tear, if they unstitch, they unstitch. And the Rambam says he rips them off.

MALKA. So what's it got to do with us if some woman had an affair a thousand years ago?

SHMULEY. So, he uncovers her hair. And she's married. So from this we learn that married women always covered their hair.

RIVKA. And that's why? It's not cos of modesty?

DAVID. No, and the word, *parah*, doesn't even always mean '*uncovers*'. It can mean '*dishevels*', so we could say all married women had neat and tidy hair. Or it can mean '*unbraids*', so –

MALKA. I could have had plaits.

RIVKA. So why did the rabbis pick that meaning?

DAVID. They picked that meaning *then* but now it could be different.

RIVKA. Yeah, they could make another rule that's difficult for women.

SHMULEY. Rivka.

RIVKA. Rubber swimming caps, maybe, like Mrs Fishbein says.

SHMULEY. Mrs Fishbein, thank God, doesn't make Jewish law.

RIVKA. I wanted to wear my wig. I've had three fittings, it's perfect. The wedding's on Sunday.

MALKA. Rivka, see if you can find some whisky for your dad and David.

RIVKA *exits*. SHMULEY *sighs heavily*. MALKA *turns to* DAVID.

Go talk to her. She's upset. Go.

DAVID *exits*.

And you: stop worrying. Everything is fine. She's almost at the *chupah*!

SHMULEY. That's why I'm worrying. When I was twenty-one I was experimenting, getting my heart broken, not getting married.

MALKA. What's so good about getting your heart broken?

SHMULEY. I spent a summer in Italy. I went to all these dusty churches, looking at the frescoes.

MALKA. You want Rivka to look at pictures of Jesus?

SHMULEY. She's so angry. You hear these stories; rabbis' daughters who rebel. They take drugs, they run wild...

MALKA. Rivka's not running anywhere. She wants to get married. She's a good girl. Not like the Kandels' son, with the *shiksa* wife and the tattoos.

SHMULEY. She seems nice, his wife.

MALKA. She smiles but she wears the trousers. She wouldn't let him circumcise the boys. She takes them to church.

SHMULEY. Well, they're coming to *shul* for *Shabbes*.

MALKA. They're going to come to us for *Shabbes* and go to church on Sundays?

SHMULEY. I didn't ask.

MALKA. They have to choose. You can't dance at two weddings at the same time. The community will never accept them.

   DAVID, RIVKA *and* LEELA *enter, with a bottle of whisky and shot glasses.* DAVID *is excited.*

DAVID. Shmuley, Leela says the vow they make is to sacrifice their beauty, not their hair. That's what they say. They don't say 'hair'.

SHMULEY. They don't say 'hair'?

DAVID. We might be all right, you know? It might not be idol worship. We might be fine.

SHMULEY. You're right! *Baruch Hashem*, we can forget this *mishigas*.

RIVKA. Really? I can wear the wig?

LEELA. What idol worship?

   The phone rings. MALKA *exits.*

DAVID. The bit in the temple.

LEELA. But we don't worship idols.

MALKA enters.

MALKA. Alan Baum. He sounds upset.

SHMULEY. The man survives on only fruit; of course he's upset.

SHMULEY exits.

DAVID. But there's this picture here. This big golden idol.

RIVKA. And in your kitchen you've got those…

LEELA. They're just to focus. Like, you can look at a flower or a leaf. A chair. A jar of Marmite. It's just to help you imagine. It isn't idol worship.

DAVID (*pleased*). You see? It's not even idol worship!

SHMULEY enters.

SHMULEY. The decision came. It's on the internet; can you look? Alan Baum says there's a list. Which wigs are Indian hair. Is it there, David? Can you see it?

RIVKA. But you said it might be okay.

SHMULEY. So now the decision came. Is it there?

DAVID. It's here. (*Reads.*) Freda, Jacquelyn, First-lady (blended), Melanie, Jaffa Natural –

SHMULEY. They name the wigs?

MALKA. Yours is a Melanie, isn't it, Rivka?

RIVKA. Yeah, mine's a Melanie. Yours is a First-lady (blended).

MALKA. I knew I should have got a Rosalyn.

DAVID. I'll call my dad.

He exits. MALKA slumps into a chair, deflated. SHMULEY gets a bucket, tears out pages of the magazine and throws them in. He gets out matches. He takes the wig off the styrofoam head.

LEELA. Is this why you can't eat in my house, Riv?

RIVKA. No. Dad, wait a second –

SHMULEY (*still tearing pages*). It's better, Rivka.

LEELA. You can't wear my clothes.

RIVKA. That's not about –

LEELA. Cos I might have worn them near the 'idols'?

RIVKA. No, that's mixing wool and linen – Dad! No!

He puts the wig in the fire. She pulls it out of the flames.

SHMULEY. You'll burn your fingers!

LEELA. My mum sacrificed her hair cos she was desperate, cos
she had nothing else to give, and now you want to burn it in
a bucket. It's not complicated.

She exits.

RIVKA. Leela!

She exits, taking the wig with her. MALKA *gives*
SHMULEY *a look.*

SHMULEY. What can I do? We got the decision.

MALKA. Does it say to burn them?

SHMULEY. Everybody's doing it.

MALKA. So if they jump off a cliff, will you follow them?
What if it's like the broccoli?

SHMULEY. That was broccoli and this is idol worship!

MALKA. Just wait till tomorrow, don't do something extreme
and regret it later.

DAVID *enters.*

DAVID. My dad's having a bonfire.

SHMULEY. You see?

DAVID. He's doing it tonight. He said if you want to go there,
you're welcome.

SHMULEY. What for to go to his bonfire? We should make our own bonfire.

MALKA. At this time of night? You want to call the whole community?

The phone rings in the hallway.

SHMULEY. The whole community's calling us!

MALKA. Like the Takhana Merkazit in here.

She exits. RIVKA enters.

RIVKA. She wouldn't listen. She just got on a bus.

DAVID. She'll understand.

RIVKA. I don't even understand! And she's not the only Hindu who's going to get pissed off.

MALKA enters.

SHMULEY. So you want to start worshipping idols just so we don't offend people? Take off the wig, Malka. You must have a *tichel* in the house. It's *avodah zara*.

MALKA. All these years I've been wearing it, it's been *avodah zara*.

SHMULEY. So we didn't know before.

MALKA. Some people are saying widows don't even need to cover their hair.

SHMULEY. A widow and a married woman are the same.

MALKA. It was in the *Jewish Chronicle*! We don't have husbands to keep us warm at night.

SHMULEY. It said that in the *Jewish Chronicle*?

MALKA. No: I'm asking you. Why are they the same? If God doesn't want me to wear my wig, so I won't wear it!

She pulls her wig off.

SHMULEY. Malka!

MALKA. Wonderful hair, I had. It's ruined now.

SHMULEY. Malka, David's here!

MALKA. I want to feel the wind blow through what's left of it.

She exits, holding the wig.

SHMULEY. Like that she's going in the street?

The front door slams. SHMULEY *makes a gesture of frustration and exits.*

DAVID. My dad wants us to come to the bonfire.

RIVKA. You said it might be okay, David. You said the law might change.

DAVID. Yeah, I was hoping.

He goes to pour himself a glass of water. He murmurs a blessing. He drinks.

RIVKA. This is what I was going to look like for you.

He looks round to find that she's put the wig on.

DAVID. Don't put that on, Rivka!

RIVKA. Don't you like it?

DAVID. You've got an idol sitting on your head. Rivka.

RIVKA. Look how upset you are; maybe you should have become a rabbi like your dad and his dad and –

DAVID. Take it off. Please.

RIVKA. You think you're such a rebel becoming an optician!

DAVID. Rivka, let's take it to my house. People will see it burn, they'll know we've done it.

RIVKA. I don't care if people know or people see!

DAVID. Okay then: I'll go.

RIVKA. But we're talking.

DAVID. You're shouting at me, Rivka.

RIVKA. So shout back. Say something.

DAVID. I can't talk to you like this.

He leaves. Infuriated, she unbuttons the top of her blouse and pushes her sleeves up. The sound of his car driving off. A moment and then MALKA *and* SHMULEY *enter.* MALKA*'s holding her wig, her hair still free.*

SHMULEY. Where's David gone? Why are you wearing that?

RIVKA. We had an argument.

SHMULEY. Such an argument he didn't even stay for coffee?

The phone rings again. MALKA *doesn't move.* SHMULEY *sighs and exits.*

MALKA. That phone's going to kill us tonight.

RIVKA. Did you feel the wind blow through your hair? How was it?

MALKA. Cold.

SHMULEY *enters, putting on his coat.*

SHMULEY. Susie Abrams. I completely forgot. I said I'd check her *mezuzot.*

He shrugs, and exits.

MALKA. Why don't you take it off? It's tight, the way the combs grip. It gets hot. Take it off. I forgot how nice it feels to have your hair free. I used to be able to sit on my hair. Yeah, I forgot a lot of things. Wait.

She exits. She enters with a bottle of vodka, brushing the dust off it with her sleeve.

We should dust inside that sideboard. I'm ashamed. Come on.

RIVKA. Me?

MALKA. You think I drink vodka every night? When we were young, we drank anything. My father used to boil potato peelings. (*She pours.*) *L'chaim.* To your wedding.

She murmurs a blessing and clinks glasses with RIVKA. MALKA *drains hers.* RIVKA *hesitates, murmurs a blessing,*

sips hers and coughs. MALKA *laughs at her. She pours
herself another shot, raises her glass.* RIVKA *bursts into tears.*

Don't cry. Ssshhh, Rivkele. You don't know: the best thing
about an argument is afterwards you make up.

RIVKA. But what if we don't make up…?

MALKA. Of course you'll make up… Rivkele, don't cry…
What's wrong?

RIVKA. David touched me, and I didn't feel anything.

MALKA. David touched you? Before the wedding?

RIVKA. I had something in my eye. He got it out. I didn't feel
anything.

MALKA (*laughs*). He touched your eye and from that you want
fireworks? Let him really touch you! *After* the wedding!

RIVKA. But Patrick…

MALKA. The tree-hugger? Did he upset you? I'll kill him.

RIVKA. No. He – he picked my hair up. Held it. Like, to see
how heavy it was.

MALKA. He weighed your hair?

RIVKA. No. He just… held it.

MALKA. *Nu?*

RIVKA. I liked it.

MALKA. For this you twist my head? Better to cry if you
didn't like it. Some women don't like being touched. They're
cold in bed, their husbands go with other women, they end
up old and bitter –

RIVKA. But Patrick's not my husband.

MALKA. So, you liked it with him, you'll like it with David
even more. You love David.

RIVKA. David told me some weird story about how we don't
know anyone but we have to marry them anyway. What if I
don't know him?

MALKA. Years you've known David! I hardly met my husband before the wedding.

RIVKA. Was it okay? When you touched for the first time?

MALKA. It was no picnic! But I barely knew him! It will be different with you. You'll have your own flat, you'll make your own friends, new friends, better friends.

RIVKA. What's wrong with my friends?

MALKA. I like Leela. But she's different. She brings this boy into the house...

RIVKA. She's my best friend.

MALKA. Look at you, so worried! You think no one got last-minute nerves before?

RIVKA. Did you?

MALKA. More than nerves I had. I was a scandal!

RIVKA. But I've never heard about it.

MALKA. Everyone who ever knew about it is dead. That's what happens when you're old.

RIVKA. But what kind of scandal?

MALKA. Can I tell you? (*She drains her glass. She pours another drink.*) Now we can talk like old married ladies. I never felt old enough to be a grandmother. Old married ladies!

RIVKA (*doubtfully*). Old married ladies.

MALKA. I was in love with someone else, that's what scandal. She had red hair to her waist –

RIVKA. You were in love with a girl?

MALKA. Such a girl! Her eyes were green, like grass.

RIVKA. But did people know?

MALKA. They found out. We were in the synagogue. Her tongue was in my mouth, my hand was on her breast. The caretaker came in. He talked and talked till I couldn't show my face in the street. One night, she came to me. She'd stolen a bike. She said she'd put me on the handlebars and we'd be miles away by morning. (*Little pause.*) Sometimes I think, since I didn't get on that bike, my life is *oysgevapt*.

RIVKA. I don't know what that means...

MALKA. Like champagne when the bubbles go. No fizz. Just nothing. Flat.

RIVKA. So why didn't you go with her?

MALKA. I was married! I was pregnant with your mother!

RIVKA. But what about the girl you loved?

MALKA (*pushing the bottle away*). For that my parents walked across Russia? And, thank God, your grandpa was a *mensch*, he took me back. Men like that you don't find every day.

RIVKA. But if your life was *oysgevapt*...

MALKA. My life has children, grandchildren, a community, a home. She lost everything. Her family sat *shiva* for her. Tore their clothes. She had to go and live in Earls Court!

RIVKA. What's so bad about Earls Court?

MALKA. I made a decision and I never looked back. People talked enough as it is! But, *Baruch Hashem*, they died, and the talk died with them. This won't come back on you.

RIVKA. I'm not worried about me.

MALKA. That's right; you are going to be a bride. My head is swimming.

RIVKA. Do you want some water?

MALKA. No, I'll go to bed. (*She gets up.*) You'll call David tomorrow, you'll make up, you'll see. (*Hearing a car pull in.*) Good; your dad's back. I thought Susie Abrams would talk his head off. She's lonely, poor thing. (*Taking the bottle.*) I'll put this away. Night, Rivkele.

RIVKA. Night, Grandma.

MALKA *exits.* SHMULEY *says:* '*Night, Malka,*' *in the hallway and enters, touching the* mezuzah *and kissing his fingers.*

SHMULEY. Do me a favour, take that wig off now. And call David; you'll feel better.

RIVKA. How do you know if you love someone, really love someone?

SHMULEY (*sighs*). I wish your mother was here. She'd know what to say.

RIVKA. She isn't. There's just you.

SHMULEY. Why do we break a glass at the wedding?

RIVKA. Dad...

SHMULEY. Come on; you know this.

RIVKA. To remind us even when there's joy, there's also pain.

SHMULEY. And wouldn't it be nice to forget? To just be joyful? But the world isn't perfect, the world is shattered. There's always pain, there's always doubt.

RIVKA. But what if he's not 'The One' for me? What if he changes? Or if I do? What – ?

SHMULEY. Rivkele, these questions; they're not questions another person can answer.

RIVKA. But I need –

SHMULEY. Ssshhh. (*He puts his hand on her head to bless her.*) Yesimech Elohim ke Sarah, Rivka, Rachel ve Leah. Yevarechecha Adonai veyishmerecha. Ya'eir Adonai panav eilecha veechuneka. Yisa Adonai panav eilecha, veyaseim lecha shalom.

RIVKA. I don't feel peaceful.

SHMULEY (*laughs*). You're not meant to; you have to struggle, to think, to doubt. Otherwise it's blind faith, and who wants that? Not God. (*He kisses the top of her head.*) Night, Rivka.

He exits. She stands in the middle of the kitchen. She whirls slowly around, not knowing where to go. Lights down.

End of Act One.

ACT TWO

Scene One

*Very late that night. The wood. PATRICK and RIVKA are on a
small platform high in an oak tree. It's made out of skinny
branches, blue polypropylene rope and blue tarpaulin, and
looks a bit like a bird's nest. The branches creak, birds sing, a
woodpecker drills, frogs croak, leaves rustle. Ivy winds around
the tree. Perhaps the ground, thirty feet below, is visible, with its
carpet of bluebells. From another tree come sounds of the other
tree-sitters, playing the guitar, drums, laughing. RIVKA, still in
the wig, has unbuttoned the top of her blouse, and pushed her
sleeves up. PATRICK is splattered in mud. They have almost
finished a bottle of kosher wine, which they are drinking out of
bashed-up tin mugs.*

PATRICK. You get drunk fast, don't you?

RIVKA. I'm not drunk.

PATRICK. No? We'd better fill you up. (*He sees that the bottle
is empty.*) What *was* that stuff?

RIVKA. I took it from the house.

PATRICK. Well, I've got beer. Let's get mangled.

*He opens two bottles of beer, passes one to her and takes a
swig from his. He gets out a pack of Bourbon Creams.*

And Bourbon Creams. Don't say I didn't wine-and-dine you.
I hope you're a twister not a dunker cos I can't be arsed with
going down the firepit for tea.

RIVKA. A twister?

PATRICK. You know.

RIVKA. No…

PATRICK. Okay: the world splits into two kinds of people. One lot dunk their Bourbon Creams. Me, I'm a twister.

He shows her, slowly, flirtatiously.

You twist off the top biscuit. Just eat that. Now you take the other biscuit. Lick the cream off. Eat it. Now, doesn't dunking seem a waste?

He holds out a biscuit; a kind of challenge.

RIVKA. I'm... not hungry.

PATRICK. Bollocks. You're a waif.

A moment of anxiety where she holds the biscuit. Then she wolfs it down, takes a huge gulp of beer and almost immediately panics. She leans forward and puts her fingers down her throat.

What are you doing?

He pulls her fingers out of her mouth and takes hold of her arms.

RIVKA. I can't. I shouldn't have. I'm sorry.

PATRICK. What?

RIVKA. The beer, the biscuit, I look like a slag...

PATRICK. You what?

RIVKA (*pulling down her sleeves*). You can see my collarbone, my elbows –

PATRICK. Yeah. I'm going crazy looking at your elbows. Drink some water. Water's okay, isn't it? They don't stop you drinking water.

She buttons her blouse to the top. He gives her some water. She murmurs a blessing over it and drinks it.

RIVKA. I'm sorry.

PATRICK. It's not a 'sorry' thing. Just breathe, all right?

RIVKA. I'm breathing.

PATRICK. Keep doing that.

RIVKA. I'm sorry –

PATRICK. Breathe.

RIVKA. No, but I –

PATRICK. Ssshhh.

Pause. He drinks some beer. He passes her bottle back to her.

Come on. It's better than that minging kosher wine.

She says a blessing and then drinks some beer. He passes her a biscuit, which she says another blessing for, before eating it the way he showed her. He watches. She takes a deep breath. She laughs.

There you are: you've crossed the line. I saw this coming when we met. I thought: 'She's not like that.'

RIVKA. Really? Did you think that?

PATRICK. Sure. And doesn't it feel good, doing what you want?

RIVKA. I feel like Leela.

PATRICK. Leelavathi doesn't do what she wants in the open. She doesn't have the guts.

RIVKA. Yeah, cos of her mum.

PATRICK. No, she gets off on it. The thrilling secrecy. Like having an affair.

RIVKA. It's hard for her.

PATRICK. Harder for you and look how far you've come.

RIVKA. Look at me freaking out when I break the rules.

PATRICK. Fuck the rules. What do you need them for?

RIVKA. But if everyone just did what they wanted – aren't you scared of chaos?

PATRICK. I'm scared of all that boiling-water shit you do. I mean, up here, doesn't it feel like people making life complicated?

RIVKA. It does seem very far away.

PATRICK. See that silver streak? The badgers come out at night...

RIVKA. Oh, yeah.

They look down into the wood. A moment of stillness and then from another tree comes a shout. The drumming stops. PATRICK *listens as the tree-sitters shout, variously:* '*Firepit!*' *then:* '*Now!*' *and then:* '*Come on!*'

PATRICK. Just a sec.

RIVKA. But –

He exits down the rope ladder. The guitar playing stops and there is the sound of frantic movement as all the tree-sitters climb down and meet by the firepit. RIVKA *tries to see what's going on, but she can't. After a moment,* PATRICK *enters.*

PATRICK. You're going to have to go, Rivka.

RIVKA. But you said I could stay.

PATRICK. We got a tip-off; they're evicting us, in the morning.

RIVKA. I don't understand...

He has been moving stuff around the tree house, working quickly and efficiently. Now he gets out a bicycle D-lock.

PATRICK. The yellowjackets are coming. The men with chainsaws. You've missed the last Tube but there's a bus. It takes for ever but –

RIVKA. What's the bike lock for?

PATRICK. Locking on the tree. (*Showing her.*) Round my neck and this branch here. They'll need bolt croppers to get it off. A Kango hammer and an angle grinder for the rest. They won't be getting me out in a hurry. Come on, I'll point you in the right direction.

RIVKA. Can't I stay here?

PATRICK. Trust me, you don't want to do that.

RIVKA. But I could help.

PATRICK. If you want to volunteer back at the squat, I can get
you on the phone tree.

RIVKA. But I'm here now.

PATRICK. Don't tell me a couple of hours up a tree's made you
fall in love with it.

RIVKA. I just want to stay. You're all staying.

PATRICK. We know how to handle ourselves.

RIVKA. I won't get in the way.

PATRICK. You don't want to get arrested, do you? I can just see
your granny picking you up from the police station.

*He turns to empty his bag. It is full of soya-milk cartons. She
takes the D-lock and locks it around her neck and the
branch, slipping the key down her bra.*

Jesus, Rivka! What are you trying to do?

RIVKA. I'll stay with the tree, I won't let them cut it down.

PATRICK. It's going to get rough, Rivka.

RIVKA. I don't mind.

PATRICK. It's not a question of not minding. I've been hit with
a baseball bat before now, I've had my arm broken. And they
don't play nice if you're a woman. Do you want to get
slapped in the face? Dragged out of a tree? Do you want
them grabbing at your tits and pulling your hair? Where's the
key?

He advances. She shrinks back against the tree.

RIVKA. I can't go back. I can't go home.

PATRICK. Why not?

RIVKA. I've crossed a line.

PATRICK. You only ate a Bourbon Cream!

RIVKA. I'm up here with you in the middle of the night.

PATRICK. I never asked you to come.

RIVKA. Don't you want more people here? If I stayed here then you could save another tree.

PATRICK. This isn't your tree! Do you even know how old it is? What kind of tree even?

RIVKA. Is it an oak?

PATRICK. Lucky guess.

RIVKA. How old is it?

PATRICK. Five hundred years. At least. You just turn up.

RIVKA. I'll look after it for you. I promise. The more people you've got, the more trees you can save.

PATRICK. I don't know...

RIVKA. Think about it.

> RIVKA *reaches for the bottle of beer. She sips it.* PATRICK *watches her as she goes for the biscuits next, and starts eating.*

PATRICK. If you stay, you're not my responsibility.

RIVKA (*her mouth full*). That's fine.

PATRICK. If something happens –

RIVKA. Don't worry.

PATRICK. I'm not worrying; I'm telling you. The only point you being here is if it frees me up, so you'd be on your own.

RIVKA (*downs the beer and smiles at him*). Can I have some more?

PATRICK (*laughs*). I can't believe you've talked me into this.

> *He opens a bottle of beer for her. The sounds of activity have calmed a bit. The guitar starts again.*

RIVKA. Thanks.

She leans back against the tree. She gulps down the fresh air. He watches her.

PATRICK. You can unlock yourself. They won't be here till morning.

RIVKA. I'm okay.

PATRICK (*laughs*). You don't trust me.

RIVKA (*laughs*). No.

PATRICK (*amused*). That's right. I wouldn't.

RIVKA. I've never seen so many stars.

PATRICK. You don't in the city – all the wasted light. Half of Britain's children have never seen the Milky Way. Can you believe that?

RIVKA. I don't think I've ever seen the Milky Way. I've never even climbed a tree before today.

PATRICK. Not even when you were little?

RIVKA (*shakes her head*). When I think of my family, I think of us in small dark rooms.

PATRICK. I'd go mad in a small dark room.

RIVKA (*intense*). Yeah.

A charged pause and then he moves away, with a laugh.

PATRICK. I thought you were going to kiss me just then.

RIVKA. Don't laugh at me.

PATRICK. You look so serious.

RIVKA. I don't know how to kiss.

PATRICK. You've never been kissed? That fiancé of yours; has he never…?

RIVKA. Not allowed.

PATRICK. Yeah, but –

RIVKA. I've never even held his hand. I don't know what it would feel like to hold hands... with a man...

She stretches out one hand to touch him but he is just out of reach and stays that way.

PATRICK. I don't want to fuck things up for you. (*Laughs.*) I'm not that kind of anarchist.

RIVKA. You won't... mess things up.

PATRICK. This is a bad idea...

RIVKA. You touched my hair. I want you to kiss me.

He leans across and kisses her. She kisses back. He stops. He looks at her, unsure. She rips her wig off and throws it out of the tree. He laughs. She puts her hand on his chest, keeps it there. Lights down.

Scene Two

Early the next morning. The tree. RIVKA is asleep under a blanket. She is no longer locked to the tree. From far away comes the sound of a bulldozer approaching. Then chanting begins, from below and around them; starting in a straggly way and building until it is coming from most of the tree-sitters: 'The land's not inherited from our fathers; it's borrowed from our children.' She wakes, alarmed to find herself alone. She scrambles into her clothes, under the blanket. PATRICK appears, head-first, at the top of the ladder, his face painted with tiger stripes. He roars at her. She laughs.

PATRICK. Hey, Sleeping Beauty. Do you want coffee? Oh, and paracetamol. I'm in a state of disrepair. That wine of yours. You don't take sugar, do you? Sweet enough.

RIVKA. Thanks.

He passes her a thermos flask. She murmurs a blessing before drinking. She takes some paracetamol. He gets out a pair of handcuffs. She looks alarmed.

PATRICK (*laughs*). They're for the lock-on.

RIVKA (*laughs*). Oh! I thought...

PATRICK. I know what you thought. Butter wouldn't melt in your mouth, huh? I've got some clothes for you from Tinkerbell. Stuff you can move about in.

He chucks a pair of ripped jeans and a jumper at her.

RIVKA. Thanks.

As PATRICK *continues his preparations, she tries to put the jeans on under her skirt. He looks round and laughs.*

PATRICK. I've seen it all before.

RIVKA. I know.

But she stays turned away from him, changing as modestly as she can.

Is that a bulldozer?

PATRICK. Yeah. They'll use that for the smaller trees, just knock them over. They'll have the chainsaws going all day on the bigger ones. They won't even use the wood for paper, pulpwood, firewood; they'll just burn it, you'll see. It's enough to break your heart.

A POLICEMAN'S VOICE *comes through a loudspeaker.*

POLICE. You may be committing an offence of obstruction of the highway.

The other tree-sitters whoop and blow whistles.

PATRICK (*calling, sarcastic*). Hooray!

POLICE. I will now give you a reasonable time to dismantle your equipment and leave the area. If you are still here after that reasonable time, you may be liable to arrest.

PATRICK. I should've got us whistles.

The tree-sitters whoop and whistle louder.

POLICE. Can we do anything reasonable to help you change your mind to leave this site?

PATRICK (*shouting*). Stop the road!

The other tree-sitters echo this. Another tree-sitter starts playing bongo drums. Others join in on a guitar, recorder, etc.

POLICE. You are making yourselves liable to arrest. I repeat: we will have no choice but to arrest you.

Whatever else he says is drowned out by the tree-sitters. PATRICK *gives* RIVKA *some face paint.*

PATRICK. It's not much of a disguise but it looks good for the cameras. (*Calling out.*) Ladders!

This is echoed across the wood: 'Ladders! Ladders!' PATRICK *pulls up their rope ladder.* RIVKA *starts painting her face.* PATRICK *gets out her wig. It's muddy and has leaves stuck in it. He puts it on. He flicks it.*

What do you think, is it me?

This echo of LEELA *makes* RIVKA *burst into tears.*

RIVKA. How can you?

PATRICK. What's wrong all of a sudden? (*Pause, as she cries.*) If you don't tell me, I can't help you.

RIVKA. Leela.

PATRICK. Stop that, you'll get streaks.

He takes the face paint off her.

RIVKA. I've fucked everything up.

She is still crying. He takes off the wig and holds it out to her.

PATRICK. Take it, go on. Go home.

RIVKA. I can't.

PATRICK. It's just a bit of mud. Take it.

He presses the wig into her hands.

RIVKA. I can't go home.

PATRICK. So go to Leelavathi's.

RIVKA. I can't. You're her boyfriend.

PATRICK. She knows I don't believe in tying people down.

RIVKA. But she's in love with you.

PATRICK. This kind of thing doesn't fuck people up; it's secrets and lies that do that. (*Pause*.) It was beautiful last night.

RIVKA. I was shit...

PATRICK. You were perfect.

RIVKA. No.

The bulldozer now sounds much louder, much closer.

PATRICK. Rivka. If you want to go then I can lock on here. But you need to decide now.

RIVKA. No. It's okay. (*She holds out the wig*.) You wear the wig.

PATRICK. It's liable to get trashed.

RIVKA. Doesn't matter.

He puts the wig on, then a climbing harness. The loudspeaker comes in again.

POLICE. This is your last warning. You will be liable to arrest for offences including aggravated trespass...

The whistling and whooping starts up again, drowning him out.

RIVKA. What tree will you be in? Can I put your number in my phone?

PATRICK. No phones, love; the police.

RIVKA. But –

PATRICK. Okay: some stuff to know. That's your first line of defence. Stab a knife in a soya-milk carton and it's like a water pistol but better cos it dries on and it reeks. If they get violent, be as visible as you can. Mustardseed's going to be down there with a video camera, so if they assault you in plain sight, we'll take them to court. There's food there, coffee. Flapjacks.

He pockets a flapjack. A chainsaw starts up. He flinches.

The chainsaws go right through you, don't they?

RIVKA. Yeah.

PATRICK. Here's cushions and a blanket. Get as cosy as you can. And here's your lock.

The chainsaw continues. RIVKA *locks on to the tree.*

RIVKA. Where will you be, though?

The loudspeaker starts up again.

POLICE. We can now consider that a reasonable amount of time has elapsed.

The whistling and whooping starts up again.

PATRICK. Fuckers.

He joins in the whooping, which is almost drowning out the sound of the POLICEMAN'S VOICE.

POLICE. You are now liable to arrest. Let me be clear: you are now liable to arrest.

RIVKA. Patrick…

There is a crack and then a sickening creak, and a tree crashes to the ground. The whistling and whooping stops.

PATRICK. Makes you sick, doesn't it? Rips into your stomach…

RIVKA. I just want to know where you'll be… in case…

He squats down beside her.

PATRICK. You taking care of this tree means I can go all over. That JCB might just grind to a halt. The chainsaws might develop faults. You didn't hear this from me; if anybody asks, the pixies did it.

The chainsaw starts again, on another tree. PATRICK *stoops and kisses her on the forehead.*

Bless you for doing this. You've got guts.

He exits. The sounds of the bulldozer and chainsaws get louder and closer.

POLICE. We must ask you to leave the area. We must ask you to come down out of the trees.

The other tree-sitters whoop and whistle over this. RIVKA *reaches into her coat and gets out* OK! *magazine. She tries to read. The whoops and whistles die down and are replaced by one of the tree-sitters, shouting: 'Take it easy! Leave him alone, you coward!'* RIVKA *looks up, terrified. She forces herself to go back to the magazine. She flicks over the pages. Another tree comes down with a cracking and creaking. The bulldozer rumbles on. Wisps of smoke starts to waft into the tree house.* RIVKA *starts coughing and looks around, terrified. Her hand goes to the D-lock. Then she takes a deep breath and covers her eyes with her right hand. Her prayer and the action is simultaneous.*

RIVKA. Shema Yisrael, Adonai Eloheynu, Adonai Echad. (*She uncovers her eyes and whispers the next line.*) Baruch shem kevod malchuto le'olam va'ed. (*Then in her normal voice, fast, she continues.*) Ve'ahavta et Adonai Elohecha, bechol levavecha, oovechol nufshecha, oovechol me'odecha. Vehayoo hadvarim ha'eyleh, asher anochi metsavecha hayom al levavecha. Veshinantam levanecha, vedibarta bam, beshiftecha bevetecha, oovlechtecha vaderech, oovshochbecha oovkoomecha. Ookshartam le'ot al yadecha, vehayoo letotafot bein enecha. Ooktavtam, al mezuzot beitecha, oovisharecha.

There's more smoke now. RIVKA *coughs as, from below, come the sounds of tree-sitters, shouting: 'Pick on someone your own size! You big bully!' Another tree crashes down.*

Vehaya im shamo tishmu el mitzvotai, asher anochi metsaveh et-chem hayom le'ahava et Adonai Eloheichem, ool avdo bechol levavchem, oovechol nufshechem, venatati metar artzkhem bito, yoreh oomal kosh, vasafta deganecha, vetiroshecha veyitzharecha.

She coughs again at the smoke. From another tree comes the sound of one of the other tree-sitters, a woman, screaming: 'Don't touch me! Don't touch me!'

Venatati eisev besadcha livhemtecha, ve'achalta vesavata. Hishamru lachem pen yifte levavchem, vesartem, va'avadtem Elohim acheirim, vehishtachavitem lahem.

RIVKA *coughs. The woman calls out: 'Don't touch me!' and the other tree-sitters are now calling out to her: 'Mustardseed! Mustardseed!' 'Don't let the bastards grind you down.'*

Vehara uf Adonai bachem, ve'atsar et hashamayim, velo yi-heyeh matar, veha'adama lo titein et yevulah, va'avadtem meheira mei'al ha'aretz hatova asher Adonai no-tein lachem.

RIVKA *coughs. The woman from the other tree screams. Smoke is pouring into the tree house now.*

Vesamtem et devara eileh, al levavchem ve'al nufshechem, ookshartem otam le'ot al yed-chem, vehayoo letotafot bein eineichem.

RIVKA *coughs. A chainsaw starts up very loud and close.* RIVKA *covers her ears.*

Velimadtem otam et beneichem, ledabeir bam beshiftecha beveitecha, oovlechtecha vaderech, oovshochbecha oovkoomecha.

RIVKA *coughs more. The chainsaw is even louder.*

Ooktavtam al mezuzot beitecha oovisharecha. Lema'an yirbu yemeichem, vimei veneichem, al ha'adama asher nishba Adonai la'avoteichem, lateit lahem kimei hashamyim al ha'aretz.

The chainsaw sputters and then grinds to a halt. There is a second's silence. And then the tree-sitters start whooping and whistling loudly.

Vayomeir Adonai el Moshe leimor: dabeir el benei Yisrael, ve'amarta aleihem ve'asu lahem tzitzit, al kanfei vigdeihem ledorotam, venatnu al tzitzit hakanaf petil techeilet.

One tree-sitter starts to sing: 'The chainsaws, the chainsaws, they cut down all our trees. The pixies, the pixies, they trashed their JCBs.' The other tree-sitters start to join in.

Vehaya lachem letzitzit, uritem oto oozkhartem et kol mitzvot Adonai va'asitem otam, velo taturu acharey levavchem, ve'acharey eineichem asher atem zonim achareihem lema'an tizkru va'asitem et kol mitzvotai viheyitem kedoshim leiloheichem.

Another chainsaw starts up, further off. The singing continues. Smoke is now pouring into the tree house. RIVKA *is coughing throughout.*

Ani Adonai Eloheichem, asher hotseiti et-chem meyeretz Mitzrayim liheyot lachem leilohim; Ani Adonai Eloheichem... Emet.

Two SECURITY GUARDS *enter. Their faces are barely visible as they are wearing masks against the smoke, and hard hats, as well as fluorescent-yellow jackets and heavy boots.* RIVKA *stabs a knife into a carton of soya milk, hitting one of them.*

GUARD 1. Pissing shit!

She stabs a knife into another carton and gets the other one.

GUARD 2. Fucking soya.

Below, the tree-sitters are whistling and whooping, gathered under the oak tree.

GUARD 1. Come on, love, you've made your protest.

They advance on her with bolt croppers. She screams. Snap blackout.

End of Act Two.

ACT THREE

Scene One

That evening. The kitchen. MALKA *sits, tensed and alert, her hair covered by a snood. She leaps up as she hears a car arrive.* SHMULEY *and* RIVKA *enter. He touches the* mezuzah *and kisses his fingers as he comes in.* RIVKA *is in jeans, one sleeve of her blouse ripped off, exhausted, cut, bruised and caked in mud, which splatters the kitchen floor.*

MALKA. *Baruch Hashem*, you're home! (*To* SHMULEY.) You let her walk around in these *shmattas*?

SHMULEY. We drove, Malka.

MALKA. But did anyone see you, at the police station? Or when you came out of the car, was someone going past?

She moves to the window to look.

SHMULEY. It's a cul-de-sac. Who goes past?

MALKA. What happened to your arms?

RIVKA. I got dragged out of a tree.

MALKA. With the wedding on Sunday? At least the dress will cover it up. Go, have a shower, then I'll put some TCP.

SHMULEY. Let her sit down a minute, have a cup of tea.

MALKA. I just cleaned in here.

SHMULEY. Sit, Rivka.

RIVKA slumps at the table. SHMULEY *looks at* MALKA *expecting her to make the tea. She doesn't. He sighs and puts the kettle on. The phone rings in the hallway.*

MALKA. It's been non-stop.

MALKA exits. SHMULEY *opens a cupboard or two.*

SHMULEY. Has it moved, the tea?

RIVKA. No… it's there. Next to the spices.

SHMULEY. Spices… spices…

RIVKA. No, not there.

She gets up and finds the tea. She puts it on the counter. She goes and sits back down.

SHMULEY. Now, where are the mugs? (*He opens a cupboard or two.*) Found them! You want a macaroon maybe?

RIVKA. No, I'm okay.

He makes three mugs of tea, putting one down in front of her. MALKA enters with a battered first-aid box.

MALKA. Alan Baum. Again.

SHMULEY. He's driving me mad!

MALKA. Well, can you blame him? Everyone is making a decision about the *sheitels* except you.

SHMULEY. Sometimes I want to give that man a proper meal!

MALKA. I told him you're out.

The phone rings again. MALKA sighs and exits.

SHMULEY. You want some sugar maybe? Sweet tea's good after a shock…? You saw some horrible things up there…

RIVKA. Oh, Dad, you should have seen it, what they did to people. And the trees…

SHMULEY. You look different.

RIVKA. I'm a mess.

SHMULEY. No: you look… nice. And it's not your wedding day and I'm not lying.

MALKA enters, looking shaken.

MALKA. Mrs Fishbein.

SHMULEY. Tell her I'll decide when I decide!

MALKA. She didn't call about the *sheitels*. I didn't even think about it: Rivka didn't go to work today. I said she isn't well.

SHMULEY. What for to lie?

MALKA. You want me to tell Mrs Fishbein she got arrested?

SHMULEY. There's no shame in being arrested. Weren't our grandparents in Russia arrested every time they put their head out of the door?

MALKA. Not because of trees!

SHMULEY. What's wrong with trying to save a tree? The Talmud says for every blade of grass there's an angel somewhere singing 'Grow!' Rav Yohanan ben Zakkai said –

MALKA. Shmuley –

SHMULEY. If you're in the middle of planting a tree and a man comes to tell you that the Messiah has come, don't stop your work: finish planting the tree and *then* go welcome the Messiah.

Little pause.

MALKA. Well, I've said she's ill now, so that's what I've said.

Pause. She sits and starts dabbing at the cuts on RIVKA*'s arms with TCP.*

I wish we could unplug that phone.

SHMULEY. There could be an emergency.

MALKA. I know –

SHMULEY. Alan Silverstein could go at any moment, Bertha Cohen's in the hospital. Louis Berg has his *Bar Mitzvah* –

MALKA. I know, I know –

SHMULEY. – and David's calling when he finishes work.

RIVKA (*jerking away from* MALKA). Did he call? Did you say anything?

MALKA. Keep still.

SHMULEY. We told him you were out.

RIVKA. That's all?

The doorbell rings. MALKA *panics.*

MALKA. Don't answer it.

SHMULEY. Why not?

MALKA. What if it's Mrs Fishbein?

SHMULEY. She just phoned. Even she can't be in two places at once.

He exits.

MALKA. Cover yourself up, Rivka!

She takes off her cardigan and drapes it around RIVKA*'s shoulders.* SHMULEY *enters with* PATRICK, *who is as muddy as* RIVKA. *He isn't wearing the wig any more but has a woolly hat pulled down to his eyebrows. He has a bad cough.*

PATRICK. Sorry to barge in. I just came to see if you were okay.

RIVKA looks up at PATRICK and the way she looks at him tells MALKA all she needs to know.

RIVKA. I'm okay.

MALKA. It was nice of you to come and check.

To SHMULEY*'s confusion,* MALKA *moves as if to shepherd* PATRICK *out again. But* PATRICK *is rummaging in a carrier bag.*

PATRICK. I brought you this.

He retrieves RIVKA*'s wig. It's muddy, tangled, bloodstained and has leaves and twigs caught in it.*

RIVKA. Oh!

PATRICK. Sorry it's so wrecked.

RIVKA (*taking it, smoothing it out a bit*). Thank you.

PATRICK. I hope you can salvage it.

SHMULEY. You'll have some tea with us?

MALKA. Shmuley.

PATRICK (*looking at* MALKA). Nah, I should go.

SHMULEY (*putting the kettle on*). The kettle's on.

PATRICK. If it's really all right...

SHMULEY. I'm making tea! Sit. Please.

PATRICK (*sitting at the table*). Thanks.

RIVKA. What happened to the oak? Did they burn it?

PATRICK. Yeah, it's gone.

The phone rings again. MALKA *doesn't move.*

SHMULEY. Malka... I'm making tea. And according to you, I'm out and Rivka isn't well, so...

MALKA. Fine.

She exits.

RIVKA. So it wasn't any use.

PATRICK. Don't say that. You were a heroine. No one could believe it was your first eviction. You were fearless up there.

SHMULEY. My Rivkele was fearless? (*Giving* PATRICK *tea.*) Here. Drink.

PATRICK. Thanks.

RIVKA. And what about the rest of the wood?

PATRICK. Wash out.

RIVKA. No...

PATRICK. The earth's all churned up; thick mud everywhere. Tree stumps smouldering, these funeral pyres of trunks and branches. We were all crying our eyes out. Then I heard you got arrested so... I thought I'd better check. (*He breaks off to cough.*) This is burning trees all up my throat. The blackthorns. (*Coughing.*) Hazels. The wild cherry.

SHMULEY. Drink, drink.

PATRICK (*gulping tea*). Thanks. (*His cough recedes.*) They broke Acorn's leg, pulling him out of that hornbeam. Of course they're saying it's his fault. And Tinkerbell didn't get bail. But then she pixied a bulldozer...

SHMULEY. Malka, who's on the phone?

MALKA *doesn't answer so* SHMULEY *exits.*

PATRICK. Are you all right? Really?

He takes off his woolly hat. There's a nasty cut on his forehead.

RIVKA. I'm fine, but your head...

He shrugs. She puts some TCP on a bit of cotton wool.

Let me...

PATRICK. Thank you.

She starts cleaning out the cut.

RIVKA. It's deep.

PATRICK (*laughs*). Yeah, but you should see what I did to the chainsaw. Banjaxed.

SHMULEY *and* MALKA *enter.* SHMULEY *is shocked to see* RIVKA *touching* PATRICK.

SHMULEY. Rivka... what are you doing? (*Little pause.*) Stop, I'll do that.

RIVKA. It doesn't matter.

SHMULEY. Rivka? (*To* PATRICK, *as she isn't stopping.*) There's no need for her to touch you. Let me do that.

RIVKA. It doesn't matter any more.

She finishes. PATRICK *gets up, holding his mug.*

PATRICK. I'd better go. Which sink should I put this in?

SHMULEY. 'It doesn't matter any more'?

MALKA. What do you think they were doing up a tree all night?

The penny drops for SHMULEY. *He leans heavily against the kitchen counter.*

SHMULEY. How could you do this?

MALKA. What were you thinking?

RIVKA. I was thinking what you were thinking.

MALKA. No. You don't put this on me.

RIVKA. You told me your whole life was *oysgevapt*.

MALKA. I said –

RIVKA. You were in love with that girl!

SHMULEY. You told her that? You worry about talk and then you drag that story up?

MALKA (*turning on* RIVKA). I thought you were grown up enough to understand. I told you they sat *shiva* for her, I told you the shame.

SHMULEY. You kept it secret all these years, then just before her wedding you bring it to light?

RIVKA. You told me to have doubts. You gave me your blessing.

SHMULEY. Did I think you'd go up a tree with a *shaigetz*?

MALKA. I open my heart to you and this is what you do!

MALKA *exits*. PATRICK *moves to go*.

PATRICK. Okay, I… er…

SHMULEY. Just a minute. Listen to me. Whatever happened – I don't want to know what happened – do me a favour: keep it quiet. In our community, if people talk, especially about a woman, it can be the end for her.

RIVKA. Dad.

SHMULEY. What for to make a song and dance about it?

RIVKA. It's going to come out whatever you do.

SHMULEY. Why's it going to come out? He isn't going to tell anyone, are you? Whatever happened, thank God, it happened up a tree. It didn't happen in Temple Fortune, it didn't happen in Hendon. In a wood it happened! No one saw! You don't know how lucky you are. No one knows about this *mishigas*. Everything can go back to normal.

RIVKA. No it can't.

MALKA *enters*.

MALKA. Go and have a shower, Rivka. David's coming.

RIVKA (*panicking*). He's coming here?

MALKA. I put the hot water on. Go. You want him to see you like this? Go.

RIVKA *exits*. MALKA *gets out a mop and bucket*.

PATRICK. Look, I –

MALKA. Now no one can look at us and say anything is wrong in this family.

She fills the bucket with water, adds some bleach. She starts viciously mopping the floor.

SHMULEY. Was it the best idea to call him now?

MALKA. Someone has to do something!

SHMULEY. But she's a mess.

MALKA. So she's having a shower.

SHMULEY (*moving out of the way*). She doesn't know if she's coming or going.

MALKA. And where does she get that from? You're a rabbi, you're a father, you're a man. Your daughter comes to you, *farblondjet*, and you give her your blessing?

SHMULEY. I didn't know what to say.

MALKA. You never know what to say! Even with the *sheitels*! Everything is up in the air with you. Everything is 'maybe this' or 'maybe that'! You sit reading Talmud all day; no wonder your eyesight's gone. When you married my daughter, you were 20/20!

SHMULEY. So what would you have done?

MALKA. You know what your problem is, Shmuley? You made one decision your whole life and you've been worrying about it ever since! So you want to be *frum*, be *frum*! You made your bed!

SHMULEY. Who knows what it means to be *frum* any more?

MALKA. Some things we know! David's coming. The wedding's on Sunday. You tell Rivka to make up with him; otherwise you don't support her.

SHMULEY. But if she doesn't feel for him any more –

MALKA. She loves him! Years she's loved him. Now suddenly she's going to live in a tree, get her tongue pierced, stop washing her hair?

SHMULEY. Her tongue?

PATRICK. I think that's a bit of a cliché –

MALKA. Stand there. Please. Look at this mud!

SHMULEY. I *chose* to be Orthodox; she never chose this.

MALKA. She grew up with this, it's all she knows. She'd be lost without it, she'd be nothing.

SHMULEY. But you saw how upset she's been about the *sheitels*.

MALKA. Who isn't upset about the *sheitels*? Who wouldn't be upset to burn her wig? It costs a lot of money. No one's going with Jerusalem. You have to think of something.

SHMULEY. I wish we went with Jerusalem and finished.

MALKA. Stop wishing, start thinking.

SHMULEY. Think what? Rabbi Dunner says it's equivalent to eating pork. He says you can't wear any wigs from human hair. Not Indian, not European; nothing. Another rabbi says they put the hair in soap.

MALKA. So, what we can't wash now? We have to go around like *him*?

SHMULEY. Maybe!

MALKA. Why's Rivka taking so long in that shower. Rivka!

SHMULEY. She just went!

PATRICK. Look, I don't want to speak out of turn here, but –

MALKA. Don't move! It has to dry.

PATRICK. There's a whole other side to Rivka you don't know.

MALKA. We know Rivka. We know.

PATRICK. Do you know that under all those clothes she wears, she's skin and bone? Do you know that? All hollows.

MALKA. You think we want your opinion?

SHMULEY. Is he right?

PATRICK. Someone should be looking after her.

MALKA. Don't tell me how to look after my granddaughter.

SHMULEY. Okay, Malka –

MALKA. What, are you defending him now? David's coming and we need to stick together.

SHMULEY. So I've been telling him not to talk.

MALKA. He wants to keep his girlfriend. He won't talk.

PATRICK. I'll talk to Leelavathi if I want to.

MALKA. You want to break up with her, break up with her. Just don't involve my Rivka.

PATRICK. I don't want to break up with her.

MALKA. If you tell her, she'll dump you. You're not David Beckham, you know!

She tips out the bucket. RIVKA *enters, her hair wet but no longer panicking.*

Go: dry your hair.

RIVKA. We don't have a hairdryer.

MALKA. We don't have a hairdryer?

RIVKA. I always let it dry naturally.

MALKA. She lets it dry naturally!

SHMULEY. Malka, if she lets it dry, she lets it dry.

MALKA. David comes, he sees her with wet hair, he'll know she had a shower, and is that a normal thing to do, to have a shower at seven in the evening?

SHMULEY. She had to get the mud off.

MALKA. Does David know she's been up a tree?

SHMULEY. Oh. No. I see. You can't use a towel or something?

RIVKA. I'm not drying my hair, okay?

MALKA *is now scrubbing the surfaces. She finds an* OK! *magazine and stuffs it into the bin.* RIVKA *picks up the wig.*

SHMULEY. Let's put that away.

He tries to take the wig from her but she doesn't let go.

RIVKA. It's mine.

SHMULEY. David's coming; let's not shove it in his face.

RIVKA. What does it matter?

SHMULEY. You want to upset him?

RIVKA. The wig's not what's going to upset him. What did you tell him?

SHMULEY. You had an argument, you'll make up with him –

RIVKA. It's more than an argument.

SHMULEY. So far as he knows, you had an argument.

RIVKA. So you want me to lie?

SHMULEY. I want you to make up with him. Because if you don't, if you don't get married, I don't know what's going to happen.

RIVKA. Me neither!

Furious, she pulls at the wig. A moment where they all stop.

MALKA. Put it in the bin. (*Pause.*) Well, you're not going to wear it now, are you?

RIVKA *sits, holding the wig.*

SHMULEY. Rivka, when I came to this community, they whispered all the time. Because I didn't grow up Orthodox. My first day in *shul*, Sidney Katz took me aside and asked me, 'What does bacon taste like?'

PATRICK (*amused*). What did you say?

SHMULEY. 'It smells like smoke, it's chewy, then you get the salt' – it doesn't matter what I said! It took a lot to make them trust me here! The Talmud says the world's a wedding. A man's getting married. He's got the bride, the suit, the hall, the best man, but he forgets the ring and for that, he has to cancel the wedding. The rabbis say you live your whole life trying to be good, get one thing wrong and you won't make it to the world to come. Don't ruin everything at the last minute, Rivka!

RIVKA. I can't lie to him. What's he going to think on our wedding night? How can I look him in the face?

SHMULEY. Rivka: you marry David, good. You don't marry David, you can't stay here. (*Little pause.*) There, I said it.

Little pause. RIVKA *is stunned.*

PATRICK. Are you kicking her out?

The doorbell rings. SHMULEY *and* MALKA *panic.*

SHMULEY. How fast did he drive?

MALKA. Rivka, your arms!

RIVKA *doesn't move*. MALKA *tugs at* RIVKA*'s sleeves but* RIVKA *pulls away*.

SHMULEY. Am I pushing you to marry someone you don't love? No. (*Almost pleading*.) Rivkele, think about your life. Your happiness…

The doorbell rings again.

MALKA. It's not nice to make him wait.

SHMULEY. Just think, Rivka…

SHMULEY *goes to answer the door. Out in the hallway we hear not* DAVID *but* LEELA *saying: 'Hi, Shmuley.' And* SHMULEY *replies, loudly: 'Leela! Hi!' He keeps her at the door.*

MALKA (*in a whisper, to* PATRICK). Don't get any ideas. It isn't honesty to hurt someone like that. It's selfish. You think she needs this? You have to think about her now.

SHMULEY *enters with* LEELA *who starts talking, fast, the second she gets in.*

LEELA (*to* RIVKA). I've got this amazing thing to tell you. (*Noticing* PATRICK.) Oh! And you! You won't believe this. You know, last night I was all upset which, by the way, I'm sorry I got so pissed off, Riv. I mean, it's not your fault. None of you. And Riv, you were the one pulling the wig out the fire. So, I'm sorry. But also, last night –

RIVKA. Leela –

LEELA. Me and my mum started talking about the hair and stuff, and we were bonding, and suddenly she said, 'What's that blue?' Cos I forgot to reapply. The lipstick? I had a cup of tea and it came off and there's the bruise right there. So I said, 'Oh, I bashed it with my toothbrush.' Crap lie but I was improvising. But you won't believe what she said: she said, 'Oh, I hoped it was a kiss.' And I was so surprised, I mean, for her to say that. So I wound up telling her all about you. Like, totally spilling my guts out. And she was, like, fine about it. Well, not fine. First of all she said, 'Just tell me when it's over.' Then she said she hopes it's not serious but if it is serious then she'll support me. She said that! Can you imagine?

PATRICK. I can't believe you told her.

LEELA. I know! How come you're here?

A tiny awkward pause.

PATRICK. I was looking for you, wasn't I?

SHMULEY *and* MALKA *take a deep breath of relief.* PATRICK *moves to kiss* LEELA. *She takes a step back, suspicious.*

LEELA. Why didn't you call?

PATRICK. We got evicted. They threw all my tat out the tree. Don't have a toothbrush to my name. Let alone a phone.

LEELA. Did they burn down the wood?

PATRICK. Yeah.

She wraps her arms around him.

LEELA. I'm so sorry. You must be gutted. And look at your head! Did you go to A&E?

PATRICK. I'm all right…

LEELA. I'll Steri-Strip it for you. Clean it out.

The doorbell rings. MALKA *and* SHMULEY *panic.* RIVKA *instinctively pulls down her sleeves.*

MALKA. Wait!

MALKA *is brushing lint off* RIVKA's *clothes, smoothing her eyebrows, straightening her necklace.*

SHMULEY. What about her hair?

MALKA. What about her hair?

SHMULEY. You were the one worrying about her hair!

PATRICK (*to* LEELA). Let's go, babes.

LEELA. Aren't you going to answer the door?

SHMULEY. In a minute!

PATRICK. Come on, let's make tracks.

The doorbell rings again. LEELA *moves towards the door.*

LEELA. Shall I get it?

SHMULEY. No!

LEELA. Okay…

SHMULEY *exits. We hear him greet* DAVID *and then they enter.* DAVID *touches the* mezuzah *and kisses his fingers.*

DAVID. Hi. Oh, hi. I'm David.

He shakes hands with PATRICK.

PATRICK. Patrick.

DAVID (*with a laugh*). I guessed. The mud. (*To* LEELA.) Leela, I'm sorry about last night.

LEELA. No… I feel bad I got in such a strop.

DAVID. You were right! You both were. You didn't have a bonfire, did you, Shmuley? Listen, I got home to this smell of burning. Human hair. And all my sisters round the bonfire, and my mum, all in these plastic wigs. Blue, purple, silver; like a girl band. That's all he'd let them wear. And I saw it through your eyes and I hated it.

RIVKA. David –

SHMULEY. We didn't have a bonfire.

DAVID. Good, cos I think it's wrong. He's wrong. And I can't say anything because I'm an optician! (*To* RIVKA.) I *was* talking like my dad but that isn't how I'm going to be.

RIVKA. David –

DAVID. No, please: you all think he's amazing. But he can be cold. Extreme. When I left the *yeshiva*, he wouldn't talk to me. A whole year. I'm living in his house. I thought I wasn't like him but I – I close off. I put this glass wall between me and other people. Like I'm looking at them through glass, thick glass. But I'm not going to be like that any more. That isn't how it's going to be with us. It can't be right to burn a woman's hair. When we're married, in our own flat, Rivka –

RIVKA. I have to tell you something, David.

MALKA. Rivka, think.

PATRICK. Let me. Leelavathi –

RIVKA. Last night we – him and me – we slept together.

LEELA. I don't believe you.

PATRICK. It didn't mean anything.

LEELA. Oh, fuck. I never cry. (*She is now.*)

PATRICK. Leelavathi...

He tries to take her hands but she wrenches away from him.

LEELA. Don't call me that. My mum calls me that. What am I going to look like? I told her about you.

DAVID. Is it true?

RIVKA. Yeah.

DAVID. But I love you.

RIVKA. I love you too –

DAVID. You weren't going to tell me. Maybe you thought I wouldn't notice.

RIVKA. No...

DAVID. We only had till Sunday. Just three days.

RIVKA. Maybe we can still get married – maybe it's like you said, like Boaz said to Ruth, in the dark –

DAVID. Don't.

RIVKA. Cling to me like ivy.

DAVID. Rivka –

RIVKA. No, you said, you told me, we make a commitment, we don't know what's going to happen, what the future holds. I made a mistake and I've hurt you and you'll make mistakes and –

DAVID. How can I go back to my dad with this?

Little pause.

RIVKA. Okay then. Here.

She takes off her engagement ring and puts it on the table, pushing it towards him. DAVID *stares at the ring in a daze.*

MALKA (*to* RIVKA). Where are you going to go? What are you going to do?

RIVKA. I don't know.

LEELA. You all knew? And you let me come in and say all that shit.

PATRICK. I was going to tell you.

LEELA. You said you were looking for me.

PATRICK. You came out with all that stuff about your mum; I didn't have the heart.

LEELA. You didn't have the guts.

PATRICK. I'm sorry.

LEELA. I'm leaving.

RIVKA. But you have to make up with me. Leela.

LEELA. I'm not a doormat, I don't have to do anything.

She moves towards the door.

PATRICK. But they're kicking her out the house.

DAVID. What?

LEELA. Course they're not.

PATRICK. It got decided before you came.

DAVID. Rivka, what is this?

RIVKA. They wanted me to lie. Now they want, I don't know, to sit *shiva* for me? Tear their clothes? (*Turning on* MALKA *and* SHMULEY.) Is that what you want?

MALKA. You can't live in this house and one night you're up a tree and God-knows-where the next. The community will say he can't control his own daughter.

RIVKA. Dad?

SHMULEY (*turning away, choked*). I wash my hands of you.

LEELA. Give her the address of the squat.

PATRICK. The squat?

LEELA. She can't sleep on the street, can she? Just write it down for her.

MALKA. This isn't your business, Leela.

RIVKA (*to* LEELA). Thanks.

PATRICK. Er… has anyone got a pen?

DAVID. Put the ring back on. It was stupid, what I said about my dad. Forget him. It's just us now. (*Pushing the ring towards her.*) Put the ring back on.

RIVKA. It wouldn't be honest.

MALKA. 'Honest'? Not a man in a million would take you back and you worry about 'honest'!

DAVID. We can make it work.

RIVKA. You wouldn't be happy.

DAVID. I'll do whatever you want. I love you.

RIVKA. But I don't know what I want. And how can we… after I've hurt you so much?

DAVID (*in tears*). I just… I want us… You and me… I *wanted* everything to start from the beginning. I just don't know what to do.

He exits. The front door slams shut. His car starts up and rumbles off and he's gone. RIVKA *bursts into tears. She exits. We hear her running up the stairs.* LEELA *grabs a pen from a drawer and gives it to* PATRICK.

LEELA. Hurry up.

PATRICK. Right.

MALKA. Go home, Leela.

PATRICK. Don't talk to her like that.

MALKA. How should I talk to her?

LEELA. This isn't my fault.

MALKA. Who comes here, bringing music, magazines, dancing to these songs about being someone's lover, setting your spirit free –

PATRICK. Listen –

MALKA. You turn my granddaughter into a liar, lying to your mum.

LEELA. You said you were a free spirit; that was a lie!

MALKA. You bring in the outside, you bring this boy.

LEELA. I'm the one who's been fucked over here!

MALKA. You bring bad language!

LEELA. Malka –

MALKA. She was going to be married!

LEELA. You said I reminded you of you, when you were young. You said you were a rebel, a free spirit.

MALKA. I was selfish.

LEELA. You were brave.

MALKA. What's brave is when you try not to hurt people, you don't think only of yourself!

Almost unnoticed, RIVKA *enters with a small bag.*

LEELA. Not if it makes you bitter and unhappy!

MALKA. You don't know; you don't see inside my heart.

LEELA. I've been here! I've spent years of my life in this kitchen. There's marks on that ceiling from when we made fudge and it exploded. I had my first kiss at that bus stop and instead of going home to tell my mum, I ran back here to tell you. Well, now I'm going home. My mum sacrificed her beauty for me. And her hair never grew back, not the same. Not thick and glossy like it was before. To her knees. And I've spent all this time in this kitchen with you!

She grabs the address from PATRICK *and gives it to* RIVKA. *She exits, and* PATRICK *races out after her.* SHMULEY *has started emptying* RIVKA's *bag.*

SHMULEY. I want you to stay, Rivka.

RIVKA. I can't do what I want here. You said.

MALKA. Shmuley, you decided. You have to show the community you're strong.

SHMULEY. I should put the community before my daughter?

MALKA. She's turned her back on us!

SHMULEY. I already lost your mother, Rivka, am I going to lose you too?

Pause.

RIVKA. No.

SHMULEY *embraces her and brings her back in from the doorway.*

MALKA. You don't know what it's like when people talk. When they stare at you in the street.

RIVKA. Things have changed since you were young – people change.

MALKA. That's what you think.

RIVKA. So we just live for other people all the time? We never do what we want?

MALKA. If I did what I wanted, you wouldn't exist! I would have run away in the middle of the night and there would have been no Sarah, no Rivka, nothing!

She exits. RIVKA *takes a step towards the door then halts. A door slams upstairs. Pause.*

RIVKA. I thought she'd understand. Her more than you.

SHMULEY. It's hard to change. (*Beat.*) She must have really loved that girl.

RIVKA. I think she really did.

Pause. SHMULEY *sighs.*

SHMULEY. Can they fix this *sheitel*, do you think?

RIVKA. You don't want to burn it any more?

SHMULEY. Mrs Fishbein, Alan Baum; they'll all twist my head. But I'll make my own decision.

RIVKA. And it isn't right to burn it?

SHMULEY. You think I know what's right any more? Sometimes I wish God would just tell us what He wants! It's tiring, to live with doubt the whole time. It wears you out. I'm not brave like you, Rivka.

RIVKA. When you were my age, you went to war.

SHMULEY. I tried to go to war; I only made it to a chicken farm. Sometimes I think my whole life is getting there too late and meanwhile everybody else is *really* living. You live, Rivka. You really live.

She smiles at him. The phone starts to ring. He sighs and exits. Alone in the kitchen, she starts pulling leaves and twigs out of the wig, smoothing it out. Lights down.

The End.

Glossary

Amidah: a silent prayer
Avodah zara: idol worship
Bar Mitzvah: when a Jewish boy comes of age at thirteen
Baruch Hashem: thank God
Bimah: the platform you stand on in a synagogue to read the Torah
Broigus: grievance, having a grievance
Chupah: wedding canopy
Farblondjet: lost, confused
Ferkrimpter: sour-face
Frum: religious
Goyim: non-Jew
Halacha: Jewish law
Kayn eynhoreh: literally 'no evil eye', said to ward off the evil eye or jealousy
Kneidlach: dumplings
L'chaim or *Le'chayim*: 'to life', a drinking toast
Meeskeit: an ugly woman
Mensch: a good man
Mechitza: barrier separating men from women (made of flowers when at a wedding)
Mezuzah (plural *mezuzot*): a prayer in a case fixed to every doorpost in a house
Midrash: exegesis of a Biblical or prophetic text
Mishigas: madness
Mishnah: part of the Talmud
Mitzvah: good deed
Nebbish: a loser, a nothing of a person
Noodnik: nuisance, pest
Nu: so
Oysgevapt: flat, lost its fizz
Parah: a word that can mean uncovers, dishevels or unbraids
Rambam: another name for the philosopher and Torah scholar Maimonides

Rugelach: nut and raisin pastries
Shabbes: the Sabbath
Shaigetz: a non-Jewish man
Shiksa: a non-Jewish woman
Sheitel: wig
Shiva: the week-long period of grief and mourning
Shmattas: rags
Shul: synagogue
Talmud: book of discussions of Jewish law, ethics, custom and
    stories
Takhana Merkazit: Central Bus Station in Tel Aviv, Israel
Tichel: scarf used to cover hair
Torah: the Old Testament
Tzimmes: sweet carrots
Yeshiva: religious school
Zaftig: curvaceous

Shmuley's prayer on page 52 is the father's blessing for a daughter, and translates as:

May God make you like Sarah, Rebecca, Rachel and Leah. May God bless you and watch over you. May God shine His face toward you and show you favour. May God be favourably disposed towards you, and may He give you peace.

Rivka's prayer on pages 65–67 is the Shema, the affirmation of Jewish faith, and translates as:

Hear, O Israel, the Lord is our God, the Lord is One.

Blessed be the name of the glory of His kingdom for ever and ever.

You shall love the Lord your God with all your heart, with all your soul, and with all your might. And these words which I command you today shall be upon your heart. You shall teach them thoroughly to your children, and you shall speak of them when you sit in your house and when you walk on the road, when you lie down and when you rise. You shall bind them as a sign upon your hand, and they shall be for a reminder between your eyes. And you shall write them upon the doorposts of your house and upon your gates.

And it will be, if you will diligently obey My commandments which I enjoin upon you this day, to love the Lord your God and to serve Him with all your heart and with all your soul, I will give rain for your land at the proper time, the early rain and the late rain, and you will gather in your grain, your wine and your oil. And I will give grass in your fields for your cattle, and you will eat and be sated. Take care lest your heart be lured away, and you turn astray and worship alien gods and bow down to them. For then the Lord's wrath will flare up against you, and He will close the heavens so that there will be no rain and the earth will not yield its produce, and you will swiftly perish from the good land which the Lord gives you. Therefore, place these words of Mine upon your heart and upon your soul, and bind them for a sign on your hand, and they shall be for a reminder between your eyes. You shall teach them to your children, to speak of them when you sit in your house and when you walk on the road, when you lie down and when you rise. And you shall inscribe them on the doorposts of your house and on your gates – so that your days and the days of your children may be prolonged on the land which the Lord swore to your fathers to give to them for as long as the heavens are above the earth.

The Lord spoke to Moses, saying: Speak to the children of Israel and tell them to make for themselves fringes on the corners of their garments throughout their generations, and to attach a thread of blue on the fringe of each corner. They shall be to you as fringes, and you shall look upon them and remember all the commandments of the Lord and fulfill them, and you will not follow after your heart and after your eyes by which you go astray – so that you may remember and fulfill all My commandments and be holy to your God. I am the Lord your God who brought you out of the land of Egypt to be your God; I am the Lord your God. True.

A Nick Hern Book

Cling To Me Like Ivy first published in Great Britain as a paperback
original in 2010 by Nick Hern Books Limited, 14 Larden Road, London
W3 7ST, in association with Birmingham Repertory Theatre

Cling To Me Like Ivy copyright © 2010 Samantha Ellis

Samantha Ellis has asserted her right to be identified as the author of
this work

Cover image copyright © Made in Sharpedge
Cover designed by Ned Hoste, 2H

Typeset by Nick Hern Books, London
Printed in Great Britain by CLE Print Ltd, St Ives, Cambs PE27 3LE

A CIP catalogue record for this book is available from the British Library

ISBN   978 1 84842 065 6

This book is printed on FSC-accredited paper made from trees from
sustainable forests.

Amateur Performing Rights   Applications for performance,
including readings and excerpts, by amateurs in English should be
addressed to the Performing Rights Manager, Nick Hern Books,
14 Larden Road, London W3 7ST, *tel* +44 (0)20 8749 4953,
fax +44 (0)20 8735 0250, *e-mail* info@nickhernbooks.demon.co.uk,
except as follows:

Australia: Dominie Drama, 8 Cross Street, Brookvale 2100,
fax (2) 9938 8695, *e-mail* drama@dominie.com.au

New Zealand: Play Bureau, PO Box 420, New Plymouth,
fax (6) 753 2150, *e-mail* play.bureau.nz@xtra.co.nz

South Africa: DALRO (pty) Ltd, PO Box 31627, 2017 Braamfontein,
tel (11) 489 5065, *fax* (11) 403 9094, *e-mail* Wim.Vorster@dalro.co.za

United States of America and Canada: The Agency (London) Ltd, see
details below

Professional Performing Rights   Application for performance by
professionals in any medium and in any language throughout the world
(and amateur and stock performances in the United States of America
and Canada) should be addressed to The Agency (London) Ltd,
24 Pottery Lane, Holland Park, London W11 4LZ,
fax +44 (0)20 7727 9037, *e-mail* info@theagency.co.uk

No performance of any kind may be given unless a licence has been
obtained. Applications should be made before rehearsals begin.
Publication of this play does not necessarily indicate its availability for
amateur performance.